Here's How

Create High Impact Business Reports

JOYCE KUPSH

NTC LEARNINGWORKS
NTC/Contemporary Publishing Group

Originally published as *How to Create High Impact Business Reports*

Cover illustration by Art Glazer

Published by NTC Learning Works
A division of NTC/Contemporary Publishing Group, Inc.
4255 West Touhy Avenue, Lincolnwood (Chicago), Illinois 60712-1975 U.S.A.
International Standard Book Number: 0-658-00390-9

00 01 02 03 04 05 VP 19 18 17 16 15 14 13 12 11 10 9 8 7 6 5 4 3 2 1

Acknowledgments

Many people have contributed to the development of this book—my seventh book. First of all, my husband Paul has stood by me through all of my books as have my two sons Jim and Jerry, who are both employed in the business world.

Rodney Azarmi served as my graphic consultant and was always there in my times of need. Mary Buck and Kristin Kupsh provided me with many ideas and were my faithful reviewers. Two of my graduate classes gave me constructive comments and ideas.

Drs. William H. Baker and Rhonda Rhodes shared materials with me to use in the appendices. John E. Monday and Daiken Fiore each provided me with bits of technical advice. Babette Mayor developed the layout design, which was used in my last book—*How to Create High Impact Business Presentations.*

Lastly, my editor, Sarah Kennedy, provided the necessary support to make this project happen without ever losing her cheery disposition.

Joyce Kupsh

About the Author

Dr. Joyce Kupsh is a professor in the College of Business Administration at California State Polytechnic University. Her doctoral work was completed at Arizona State University in the areas of business, education, and instructional technology. Presently, she teaches presentations and facility management at both the graduate and undergraduate levels and is director of the Multimedia Design Center at Cal Poly State University.

Dr. Kupsh is a frequent speaker and has conducted seminars on a range of business topics throughout the United States and Canada. She is the author of six other books on business and design-related topics.

If you find yourself instructing others on how to create high-impact reports, the author is willing to share her instructional materials—including sample course syllabi, learning exercises, and presentations.

Dr. Joyce Kupsh
21842 Harbor Breeze Lane
Huntington Beach, CA 92646

Foreword

Success in business, as in most endeavors, requires a combination of substance and style; i.e., having something valuable to say and knowing how to say it effectively.

Perhaps this seems a truism, but this basic principle underlies all of our business communications every day. The simplest document requires both well-developed content and effective delivery. Essentially, the information explosion boils down to one basic necessity–communication. Not just making your point, but making it convincing, making it stand out from the deluge of material your audience inevitably receives. Nowhere is the need more clear than in the humble business report, the workhorse of business communication and a key component in virtually all major decision making.

Knowing that your professional success rests to such an extent on effective written communication can be intimidating. How many of us, after all, specialize in report writing? How many of us consider this a vital aspect of our role in the organization? Yet, how many of us have found achieving a major objective depended upon putting forth a well-written and professionally presented report? All of us have faced the task and will continue to face it throughout our professional careers.

Fortunately, Joyce Kupsh understands the demands of business communication. She knows the importance of displaying information in the best light through the use of effective graphics and professional formatting. She is an expert in organizing and structuring information to build a case and establish a point. And she has covered all the bases from initiating a report to polishing off the finished product. With this reference at hand, anyone can produce professional reports. And in today's communication age, that's expertise no successful business person can afford to be without.

Dr. Bob H. Suzuki, President
California State Polytechnic
University, Pomona

Table of Contents

Diagnostic Glimpse #6

How familiar are you with the desktop publishing techniques and tools available with today's computers?

Chapter 6—Designing Your Document

Introduction

Writing reports has never been a favorite task of either a student in school or a worker in the business world. Yet, the development of high-impact business reports is necessary in today's competitive, global world. *Good communication skills and the ability to write reports* are statements frequently included in the classified ads for workers.

No longer is a writer required to use a quill pen and painstakingly handwrite a report in ink or even generate a report on a typewriter making corrections using an eraser or correction fluid. Technology provides new, exciting, and better ways of doing the same old things!

Computers equipped with word processing or desktop publishing software not only make the work much easier but also provide the opportunity to enhance a top-quality report with a polished professional look. Today a writer can generate a report that equals or exceeds the look of reports of yesteryear, which required a professional team of workers—writer, typist, typesetter, and graphic artist.

Chapter 1 discusses how to plan, organize, research, and outline the report. Chapter 2 helps the writer to develop a writing style appropriate for business reports, and Chapter 3 works on polishing the writing elements and mechanics of report writing.

Chapter 4 illustrates how to give credit to other writers by either quoting or paraphrasing and selecting a reference style.

Chapter 5 gives an overview of the many types of reports, the various parts within these reports, and format ideas varying from the traditional report. Chapter 6 provides you with a foundation for designing your documents–also referred to as desktop publishing. Chapter 7 gives suggestions for finalizing your written report–or masterpiece.

This book has seven chapters for a reason. Seven is a magic number. In making a visual for a presentation, the visual should be limited to seven lines and seven words on each line. More than seven lines makes the visual cluttered. In addition, the mind cannot easily remember more than seven points. Thus, if readers are to commit to memory the information in a book, seven points is the magic number.

Consider the following examples associated with the number seven.

Things

Days of the Week
Phone Number Digits
Colors of the Spectrum
Articles in the Constitution
Kinds of Bone Fractures
Warning Signs of Cancer
Types of Love (Plato)

Groups/Events

Watergate 7
The Chicago 7
Nations of Warsaw Pact
United Arab Emirates
7 Mobsters during Prohibition Era
Women's Colleges in the East
Seven Years' War

Movies/Entertainment

The Magnificent Seven
Seven Year Itch
The Seven Dwarfs
The Seven Voyages of Sinbad the Sailor
Ages of Man (*As You Like It*)

Geographic/Religious

Seas
Continents
Hills of Rome
Wonders of the Ancient World
Sisters (Stars)
Deadly Sins
Holy Sacraments

Read the book from start to finish, or pick the chapters you most need to read first. A *Diagnostic Glimpse* precedes each chapter. This special feature consists of two pages of questions. Use it to help you determine which chapters are most vital in meeting your needs. The answers are right there in the righthand column. Just turn the book upside down to see how you did, and find out how much you know about each subject.

Read this Diagnostic Glimpse before Chapter 1.

Diagnostic Glimpse #1

Do you know how to prepare to write?

How carefully do you need to read Chapter 1, "Preparing to Write"? The questions below will help you discover how much you already know about planning, organizing, researching, and outlining a report.

Agree   Disagree   1. The first steps in preparing to write consist of planning, researching, and outlining.

Agree   Disagree   2. Developing a problem statement supported by listing purpose(s) or objectives(s) is a good way to get started.

Agree   Disagree   3. An analysis of the target audience is not necessary during the planning stage of a report.

Agree   Disagree   4. Establishing a timeline for writing a report is useless, because it can never be followed.

Agree   Disagree   5. Research is generally considered to be from either secondary or primary sources.

Agree   Disagree   6. Primary sources represent articles you find in the library.

Agree   Disagree   7. Outlining is not essential until you complete a first draft of the report.

Agree   Disagree   8. In making an outline for your report, you should not consult other people.

Agree   Disagree   9. Two or more points should be included within each subtopic of an outline.

Agree   Disagree   10. Constructing an outline is a process similar to computer programming.

1. agree
2. agree
3. disagree
4. disagree
5. agree
6. disagree
7. disagree
8. disagree
9. agree
10. agree

List five steps to use in evaluating an outline.

You have been asked to write a brief report on CD-ROM technology. Following are some thoughts or ideas on what to include. Organize the following points into a logical outline using parallel language construction with only one word for each point.

What is it?
When did it develop?
What are the various types available?
What can it do?
How is it used?
What is in store for the technology?

You are now thinking of writing a report on multimedia presentations. Arrange the following topics into three main points using subtopics for the rest of the points.

Macintosh
Windows
Future
Text
Graphics
Color
Interaction
Sound
Video
Animation
Definition
Elements
Hardware/Software Requirements

Preparing to Write

I n school, the first step in a writing assignment was choosing the topic. In business, the topic usually chooses itself, which brings you a step closer to getting the project underway.

But the next difficulty in writing remains. It is called writer's block. Often this block is caused by starting to write without proper planning, researching, and outlining. These steps are most important in creating a proper foundation prior to beginning the actual writing process.

Planning

A plan consists of a detailed scheme or method worked out beforehand for the accomplishment of an objective. The steps in forming a plan involve a systematic approach to the writing process. The steps can be divided into the following categories: analyzing the target audience, examining the budget available, setting up a time schedule, collecting the data, and establishing an organized, overall plan.

Purposes or Objectives

When considering the topic for a report, always begin by determining its purpose or objective. Sometimes it helps to think of a writing project in terms of solving

This chapter provides ideas on how to get started. These ideas include preparing to write by planning, researching, and outlining–steps that are all crucial in creating a high-impact business report. A critical part of planning and organizing involves developing an outline.

a problem. Thus, the purpose or the objective of the report is to solve the problem.

Problems to be solved may include: meeting a need for more information on a particular topic; an analytical look involving interpretation and/or recommendations; or a persuasive pitch to generate action. Chapter 5 lists examples of reports that fall into different and various classifications. Such classifications tend to build one upon the other. For example, a persuasive report will no doubt include information, interpretations, and recommendations, along with persuasive arguments for accepting or rejecting those recommendations.

Actually writing the problem statement is one way of getting started. The task of writing the problem statement is helpful in keeping both the writer and all subsequent readers in focus on the reasons for creating the report.

The problem statement should also be supported by listing purpose(s) or objective(s). While a problem statement explains *what*, purposes or objectives explain *why*. If the report has more than one problem, purpose, or objective, plan to list each of these separately. Careful planning, analyzing, and organizing allow you to provide a clear and concise problem statement and goals for your target audience.

Target Audience

Because a report needs to be written for a target audience, an analysis of that target audience is necessary in the planning stage of a report. The following questions may prove helpful in completing this task:

- What is the educational level of the intended audience?

Key Steps

✓ **Plan**

Research

Outline

- How much background or technical experience do members of your intended reading audience have on the topic?

- Is the report an upwards, downwards, or lateral communication device?

- What is the age level, gender, and nationality of the majority of the readers?

- Will the audience be expecting a formal or informal report?

- Is the report one of many or will it be one of a kind?

- Is the report expected by the readers?

- What type of action–a verbal response, a written reaction, or an interview–do you anticipate from the audience?

- Are you addressing the appropriate audience?

These questions are not a complete list but are merely intended to start your thinking regarding the analysis of your target audience. It is essential that you have a clear understanding of this group while creating the report so as to focus on their needs.

Budget

An examination of the available budget should be made before undertaking a writing project. If sufficient funds are not available, you may be wasting your time (or the company's time) by starting the project. Areas where you may require funding are:

- **Staff**–your time as well as that of any helpers you may require for research, editorial or artistic assistants, statisticians, and any other specialists (Do not assume that the report is a one-person project.)

- **Research**–fees for accessing databases, libraries, and books or periodicals

- **Supplies**–paper, duplication costs, folders or binding materials, and postage

- **Equipment**–computer (hardware), word processing/desktop publishing applications (peripherals), and/or any other specialized equipment

Time Schedule

Creating a report takes time–frequently, far more time than anticipated. A detailed timeline should be established to estimate the time necessary to complete the project–particularly if you have a completion deadline for the report.

Establishing a timeline that involves estimating the amount of time needed for each of the different steps–as well as a breakdown of time needed for work within those steps–has several merits. First, the estimate provides a step-by-step schedule to follow. Second, it establishes projected daily or weekly goals rather than one final deadline.

Even if the goals are not always accomplished, a timeline will provide an indication of where you stand. Many people find that a timeline can be an effective motivational device.

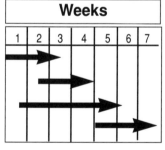

Project Timelines

Data Collection

The writer of a report seldom knows all of the information to be included. Usually, a collection of some type of data is needed. This data may be gathered from a variety of sources, known as either secondary or primary information sources. General methods of collecting the data are reviewed in the following section titled *Researching*.

Overall Plan

A likely procedure in testing a new product by Company X would be to have a time schedule, expectations, definition of tasks, definition of acceptance levels, etc. This overall plan would serve the purpose of putting everyone on the same *page* with the same agenda–important to the success of the test.

Similarly, a written overall plan should be prepared for a written project to show your commitment and your plans to achieve that commitment. Such a plan may be required by your superiors; but even if it is not, it is important as a means of reiterating your goals and purposes and organizing the project.

Researching

Research consists of a scholarly or scientific investigation or inquiry. Such research is considered to be either secondary or primary.

Secondary Sources

Secondary sources include information from books, magazines, or other publications. Someone else has already completed an investigation and has documented the information; however, you can cite (using proper reference techniques as addressed in Chapter 4) that information in support of the points that you make.

Key Steps

Plan

✓ **Research**

Outline

In addition to materials found in a library, computerized databases are a good source for locating information on a given topic. These databases are available in a number of commercial online services, such as Prodigy, CompuServe, America Online, eWorld, Internet, GEnie, and Delphi. Also, most libraries subscribe to one or more specialized data search programs.

Primary Sources

Primary sources include original data that you have obtained and compiled. Methods used to compile original data include surveys, experiments, interviews, and testing.

Surveys are conducted through written questionnaires, interviews, or observations. Experiments test one method against another. In either a survey or an experiment, a research design should be developed. A research design includes details such as sample size, sampling techniques, procedures, and statistical methods used. If you are conducting original research, a book on research design should be consulted.

Outlining

Outlining is a vital step in organizing a written project. Organization is the process of putting something together as an orderly, functional, and structured whole; outlining is the best means of achieving this orderly, functional, and structured whole.

Key Steps

Plan

Research

✓ Outline

Preparation

Before developing an outline, you may find it helpful to jot random thoughts and phrases down on paper–brainstorming. The next step is to begin to cluster these random thoughts into logical groups.

Many word processing programs contain an outline feature, which you may find helpful. However, many times a piece of paper and a pencil are sufficient and effective for developing an outline at the brainstorming stage.

If possible, involving other people may be a good way to provide more ideas and thoughts. You can do the initial brainstorming and clustering yourself before submitting a draft to another person or persons. Or, you may want to involve others in the initial brainstorming process.

Evaluation

A completed outline should meet the following requirements:

- A complete, organized list of what is to be covered in the report
- Topics and subtopics using parallel construction of words within the different levels showing a breakdown of what is to be covered
- Descriptive and functional topics and subtopics rather than attention-getting ones
- The inclusion of two or more points within each subtopic
- A parallel hierarchy of topics and subtopics

- A logical or sequential arrangement of topics and subtopics–alphabetical, size (largest to smallest or smallest to largest), time, etc.

Constructing an outline is a detailed procedure–requiring detailed skills very similar to those needed by computer programmers. Dr. William H. Baker, a professor of computer programming and business communications at Brigham Young University, has developed a process for outlining called *How to Write Structurally Sound Text*. With his permission, this procedure known as STEP (Structured-Text Evaluation Procedure) is included in Appendix C to provide details on preparing and evaluating an outline.

Creating a high-impact business report does not depend upon the topic or whether it is selected or assigned. Instead, a high-impact report is one that is favorably received and generates action. To accomplish these goals, a report must be carefully and thoughtfully designed during the initial preparation stage. Remember the longest trip can be shortened by good planning that steers you in the right direction. A well-prepared outline is the first step in the right direction.

The Bottom Line

Planning, researching, and outlining are crucial steps in creating a high-impact report. Even though the plans and the outlines may change many times during the writing of a report, they are essential if you are to know where you are going and how you are going to get there.

The next chapter explores how ideas are expressed on the written page. Your writing style is an important ingredient in determining how effective your report will be.

Read this Diagnostic Glimpse before Chapter 2.

Diagnostic Glimpse #2

How familiar are you with business writing style?

How carefully do you need to read Chapter 2, "Developing Your Writing Style"? The questions below will help you discover how much you already know about writing style.

Agree   Disagree   1. Writing style varies to fit a specific need or purpose of the writer but also reflects the personality of the writer.

Agree   Disagree   2. A business report includes facts and findings that ultimately lead to an opinion formed on the basis of those facts and findings.

Agree   Disagree   3. Reports should normally be written in first person.

Agree   Disagree   4. Long reports including many details are usually perceived as more effective.

Agree   Disagree   5. Both repetition and redundancies are encouraged to make the meaning clear.

Agree   Disagree   6. Implied ideas should always be restated.

Agree   Disagree   7. Linking the thought from one sentence to the next and from one paragraph to the next is accomplished by repeating words or by using a transition.

Agree   Disagree   8. The tone of a report can convey a positive or negative message to the readers.

Agree   Disagree   9. Writing in active voice is usually a direct and dynamic method of writing.

Agree   Disagree   10. All sentences should be similar in length.

1. agree
2. agree
3. disagree
4. disagree
5. disagree
6. disagree
7. agree
8. agree
9. agree
10. disagree

Select the better choice from each of the following:

1.　a.　crisis
　　b.　severe crisis

2.　a.　a check in the amount of
　　b.　a check for

3.　a.　last-minute reports
　　b.　reports written at the last minute

4.　a.　Mary went shopping and purchased a
　　b.　Mary purchased a

5.　a.　This example is
　　b.　This is

6.　a.　Remember to
　　b.　Do not forget

7.　a.　There are
　　b.　The report states

8.　a.　The secretary showed appreciation
　　b.　The secretary showed her appreciation

9.　a.　airline hostess
　　b.　flight attendant

10.　a.　You said that the
　　b.　The report showed

1. a
2. b
3. a
4. b
5. a
6. a
7. b
8. a
9. b
10. b

Developing Your Writing Style

Writing style refers to the way ideas are expressed on the written page. This style can vary from one individual to another reflecting the personality of the writer. Also, writing style can vary to fit a specific need or purpose.

A sincere and dedicated effort, as is the case with most skills, can improve your writing style. Consider the way professional athletes work out and practice to maintain and even increase their skills. Writing is no different. Study and practice will lead to improved performance. Whereas the mechanics of writing–discussed in Chapter 3–reflect a right or wrong way of grammar, punctuation, capitalization, etc., writing style development merely reflects a better or improved way of writing.

Numerous books and textbooks are devoted to the subject of writing style. Chapter 2 will highlight some of the key techniques needed in developing a good style. Writing style techniques that are covered in this chapter are divided into the following topic areas: objectivity, conciseness, coherence, tone, emphasis, variety, and readability.

Objectivity

Most business reports should be approached from an objective standpoint. A report is not a theme or essay reflecting personal emotions and opinions. Instead, a

Numerous business communication and report-writing textbooks are available to help individuals improve their writing style. However, the basic ideas in this chapter are designed to provide a quick overview of those writing style techniques that are particularly helpful in creating high-impact business reports.

business report includes facts and findings that ultimately lead to an opinion formed on the basis of those facts and findings.

When writing, you can maintain an objective attitude by divorcing yourself from your own personal biases and prejudices. You should try to look at all sides of the problem with an open mind before stating your conclusions. This role is similar to that of a referee at a sporting event or a judge presiding in court. In these situations, decisions are based on the results, the evidence, or an interpretation of the results and evidence–not on personal opinions and feelings.

Making it clear that you have an open mind when writing your report will, in most cases, make the conclusions and recommendations at which you arrive more believable to your readers. If a personal bias is revealed, the reader may become suspicious of the accuracy of the report. The emphasis, therefore, should be on the factual material presented and the conclusions drawn rather than on any personal beliefs.

Writing in an objective manner means using the third person–proper nouns and the occasional use of *he*, *him*, *she*, *her*, *they*, and *them*. Third-person writing is more impersonal than first person, which uses such personal pronouns as *I*, *me*, *we*, *us*, and *you*.

Impersonal writing does not mean that what you write has to be boring or dull. Most newspaper and magazine articles are written using the third person. While some of them may be exciting and interesting, others may lack luster, depending as much upon the subject as the writing style. Thus, even the blandest of topics can be positively affected through a blend of *what you say* (content) and *how you say it* (written expression of ideas).

At times, of course, you may want to make your writing more personal. If the report is a personal communication between you and your associates, for example, you may prefer the more informal approach of using first- and second-person writing by including *I, my, me, we, our, us,* and *you.* Overuse of these pronouns, however, may make you sound conceited. Thus, you may want to limit personalization and maintain a writer's sincerity rather than risk a report that may sound overbearing to your reader(s).

In any case, you need to make a decision *before* you start to write as to which style is best for the situation. Deciding at the outset on which style is appropriate for your specific needs can save considerable time and effort during the editing process.

Conciseness

Conciseness is a necessity in today's busy world; it saves time and money for both the writer and the reader(s). Long reports do not necessarily equal quality reports. Important details can be lost. Teachers may do a disfavor by assigning their students a ten-page report when the information could be adequately stated in one or two pages.

The art of being concise is difficult. Conciseness is achieved in many different ways. General categories of things to avoid in making your writing more concise follow.

Irrelevant Information

Information that is irrelevant to the report should not be included. Perhaps the reader does not need to know everything you know on the subject. Everything included in the report should be there for a reason and have a bearing on your topic and your purpose.

Redundancy

Repetition of a word can serve a purpose, but a redundancy is a useless repetition of a word. Examples of redundancies are illustrated in the following list.

> 6 p.m. ~~in the afternoon~~
> ~~free~~ gifts
> ~~important~~ essentials
> ~~basic~~ fundamentals
> ~~personal~~ opinion
> ~~falsely~~ padded expense account
> ~~severe~~ crisis
> she ~~is a female who~~

Clutter and Clichés

Clutter and clichés are frequently combined in a way that wastes words. The following examples demonstrate ways of making writing more concise.

~~Will you please arrange to send~~	Please send
~~A check in the amount of~~	A check for
~~In accordance with your request~~	As requested
~~We are not in a position to~~	We cannot
~~We would therefore ask that you kindly investigate~~	Please investigate
~~Reports that are long~~	Long reports

Extra Phrases

Extra phrases can be eliminated in several ways. First, compound adjectives help to reduce the number of words needed to express an idea. The following examples demonstrate this writing technique.

~~The writing techniques which are up to date~~
Up-to-date writing techniques

~~Reports written at the last minute~~
Last-minute reports

~~Avoid waiting until the last minute~~
Avoid the last-minute rush

A second method of eliminating extra words is by substituting a precise word or words for phrases. The following examples illustrate this point.

~~Tom was a teacher who was outstanding.~~
Tom was an outstanding teacher.

~~Writers create better output when they use a desktop-publishing package.~~
Writers using a desktop publishing package create better output.

~~The report which is incomplete~~
The incomplete report

~~Paul waited in an impatient manner.~~
Paul waited impatiently.

Implied Ideas

Implied (obvious) ideas need not be restated. For instance, the following statements can be rewritten omitting words as shown.

~~She went to school and attended class,~~
She attended class,

~~He took the test and passed it with high honors.~~
He passed the test with high honors.

~~Mary went shopping and bought a~~
Mary bought a

Abstract or General Words

On the other hand, using a single concrete word rather than a longer phrase may shorten the sentence but make the meaning somewhat vague. In reporting on the work ability of a person, words such as dependable, efficient, nice, and superior may sound good but tend to be hazy compared to more concrete, descriptive words or sentences. For instance, you could cite specific examples for each of these words.

dependable	was never late to work
	was never sick
efficient	made deadlines
	won employee-of-the month award
nice	gets along well with all employees
superior	made the highest score in a class of 200

Coherence

Coherent writing flows along without abrupt changes or, to put it another way, the writing sticks together. This cohesion is accomplished by linking the thought from one sentence to the next and from one paragraph to the next. Linking is done by repeating words and by using a transition.

Repetition

By repeating a word either directly or with a similar word, you will keep the reader aware of the topic. In the following examples, the addition of the word inserted in parentheses makes the writing stronger and clarifies the meaning. Without the inserted noun, the reader might be forced to reread the previous sentence to clarify what *this, that, these,* and *those* refer to or represent.

> This (example) will show
>
> That (task) is accomplished
>
> These (papers) will be delivered
>
> Those (plans) are the ones

Transition

Using transitions helps to blend one thought with another and aids in keeping the reader focused on the flow of the report. In a sense, they help the writing flow smoothly and bridge any gaps. Transitional words include explanation, enumeration or listing, similarity or contrast, and cause or effect.

Explanation. A transition is useful before giving an example. You can use such words as:

> also
>
> too
>
> for example
>
> as an example
>
> for instance
>
> to illustrate
>
> in the illustration

Enumeration or Listing. A transition is useful before writing a list of items. You can list items using a numbered list. However, many times the number is not important, and the items can be listed using a symbol such as • ❑ ☞ ✔ ✘ ▲ ■ ◯.

If the items are short in length or special emphasis is not needed, you may prefer to list the items within the paragraph. This listing can be done by using the numbers in this way: (1) first, (2) second, or (3) third. A semicolon should be used instead of a comma if the words in the listing include longer phrases using a comma.

Words within the paragraph are also effective in linking items. Examples are:

in addition

first

second

third

next

finally

Similarity or Contrast. Transition words work effectively in showing either a similarity or a contrast between two situations. Some helpful examples are:

Similarity	*Contrast*
likewise	in contrast
similarly	in spite of
in a similar manner	on the other hand
by the same token	however
in the same way	on the contrary

Cause or Effect. Transitional words are also helpful in showing a cause or an effect:

because of

therefore

thus

as a result

for this reason

consequently

Tone

The tone of a report can convey a message to the reader(s). Therefore, care needs to be taken to assure that the right tone is projected. Frequently, a neutral, unbiased stance is most convincing (before you conclude and recommend what you thought all along). Many different factors contribute to the tone of a message; among these are using positive versus negative and active versus passive as well as bias-free language.

Positive versus Negative

People like to hear good news; therefore, you will normally want to accentuate the positive and eliminate the negative aspect as much as possible. Exceptions can be made if you are consciously trying to dramatize a negative problem, but you need to carefully analyze the negative statements to ensure that you are making the desired impression.

Some words automatically project a negative feeling or image. For instance, the words *delay, unable, cannot, inconvenient, disappointed, broken, not,* and *unfortunately* all create an *oh dear, bad news* effect.

If, on the other hand, you want to give a positive look to bad news, a more positive word will help.

Negative	*Positive*
~~do not forget~~	remember
~~you neglected to send~~	please send
~~not honest~~	dishonest
~~cannot accept~~	unacceptable in present form

Active versus Passive

Writing in active voice–with the subject doing the acting–is usually a direct and dynamic method of writing. Yet, passive writing may be more appropriate at times. *(See the next section on Emphasis.)* Examples of active and passive writing are:

> *Active* John wrote the report.
> *Passive* The report was written by John.

Expletives

Expletives such as *there are, it is, it is noted that, it is understood that*, etc. should be either be avoided or used sparingly. Expletives are meaningless words used in beginning a sentence that tend to *muddy the water*. Even though a sentence with an expletive may be grammatically correct, the sentence is unclear and may cause the reader to look back in an effort to find to what the expletive refers. The following words may create interest in a novel but should be avoided in business writing.

Vague	*Definite*
~~there are~~	The report states …
~~it is said that~~	The research suggests …
~~it is understood that~~	The review indicates …
~~it is noted that~~	Furthermore, the results indicate …

Third Person Writing

Writing in third person (using a noun or the pronouns *he, she, him, her, they,* and *them*) is generally recommended for report writing. First person writing (using the pronouns *I, we, me, my, our, us,* and *them*) may seem to make writing more personalized, but readers may begin to think you are conceited after hearing words such as *I* or *we* too many times. Second person writing (using *you*) is recommended in letter writing in an attempt to get the attention and interest of the reader.

You should carefully consider the desired impact *before* you start writing. Since a report is more or less a factual account or summation of information, third person writing may make the final result seem more businesslike.

Thesis and dissertation writers should always write using the third person style. In a business report, you have more freedom. You may want to write the report in third person but use first or second person on occasion—such as in giving your personal recommendations and solutions. Also, a *you* now and then may personalize the report and make the reader feel more involved.

Bias-Free Language

The tone of your writing should not reflect a gender bias or any other type of bias—race, religion, age, disability, or ethnic group. Such writing can send a wrong or hidden message and may alienate readers.

Pronouns. The use of pronouns in a sentence where the gender of the noun has not been revealed shows a bias—whether intentional or not. For instance, if you use personal pronouns referring to a man as a boss and a woman as a housekeeper, you are stereotyping.

Avoid such stereotyping by avoiding the use of pronouns, changing to plural form when possible, and using pronouns from both genders. Problems and suggested corrections are:

> ~~The manager showed his appreciation~~
> The manager showed appreciation

> ~~The housekeeper is required to do her best.~~
> All housekeepers are required to do their best.

> ~~He is to report to~~
> He or she is to report to

Words. Various words and expressions show gender bias. Eliminating the use of such words and substituting a more neutral word is recommended. Even though the word *manhole* is hard to replace, many words can be stated in a more accepted version. For instance,

~~policeman~~	police officer
~~fireman~~	fire fighter
~~businessman~~	businessperson
working ~~mother~~	working parent
~~foreman~~	supervisor
~~bag boy~~	bag person
~~stock boy~~	stock clerk
~~airline hostess~~	flight attendant

Emphasis

Words placed either first or last in a sentence receive the greatest emphasis. Therefore, you should decide on your most important word or phrase and then decide whether you want that word or phrase to make an initial or a lasting impact.

Using either active or passive voice changes the emphasis of a sentence. For example, if you are portraying bad news, you may wish to write in a passive form to keep from sounding accusing.

> ~~You neglected to include the data.~~
> The data was not included.

In the following sentences, the attention is on Rodney in the first sentence. The second sentence places the emphasis on the report. If you want to give Rodney credit, place his name first. If the report being completed is more important, use the second sentence.

> Rodney completed the report.
> The report was completed by Rodney.

Variety

At times, writing rules may appear to disagree. One rule will say to be parallel, and another rule will say to use variety. Both rules are correct, but each one has its place. The hard part is deciding when to be parallel and when to use variety. In general, elements in a series—such as sideheadings, items in a series, or clauses—should be parallel.

An example of when variety is good is in the length of sentences and paragraphs. Varying the length of sentences and paragraphs breaks the monotony for the reader. Too many short sentences may make the writing sound like a first-grader's report. However, long sentences and paragraphs may put the reader to sleep. A combination will provide needed variety.

Another way of making your writing more interesting is to use variety in sentence structure. Simple sentences are easy to read but should be mixed with complex or compound sentences. Rather than beginning all sentences with the subject, you should vary the pattern and begin some sentences with a prepositional phrase

During the winter,

or a dependent clause

Because of the low budget,

If applied correctly, variety does lend interest to your writing.

Readability

The general goal of a business report is to express information rather than to impress the reader with big words and complex sentence structure. After completing a report, you may wonder if it is clear, understandable, and interesting to the readers—in other words, is it readable? Readability of a report is measured by the length of the sentences as well as the difficulty of the words.

One way of determining the readability of a report is to use a readability formula. Many different ones are available, but probably the most popular one is the Fog Index developed by Robert Gunning. Computing the Fog Index indicates the grade level of your writing. The *Reader's Digest* is written at eighth-grade level; accounting, perhaps, for that magazine's popularity. But even if you are writing for college professors, you probably want to keep reading level in the high school range.

Computing the readability level manually is a bit time consuming, so you may want to utilize a computer program to do the task. *RightWriter* and *Grammatik* are computer programs that compute reading levels automatically. These programs can also give you other types of feedback on your writing and may even provide suggestions for improvement. Use caution with these grammar checkers. Just because they flag a sentence or phrase does not mean it is wrong.

The Bottom Line

Writing style goes beyond the fundamental writing mechanics. The ideas presented in this chapter can make a difference in the overall effectiveness of a business report. Yet, the best choice of a writing style for one report may not be the best for another report. The basic ideas of writing style presented in this chapter are by no means a complete writing course, but they will certainly help you get your report underway. You may find that this quick review reminds you of many things learned and then forgotten from your school days.

The next chapter provides the fundamentals of writing by addressing the topics of abbreviations and acronyms, capitalization, italics, numbers, punctuation, spelling, and word division.

Read this Diagnostic Glimpse before Chapter 3.

Diagnostic Glimpse #3

Do you remember the mechanics of writing?

How carefully do you need to read Chapter 3, "Polishing Your Writing Mechanics? The questions below will help you discover how much you already know about abbreviations and acronyms, capitalization, italics, numbers, punctuation, spelling, and word division.

Agree Disagree   1. The image reflected by your work does not influence your readers' reaction.

Agree Disagree   2. Abbreviations and acronyms should be used with care.

Agree Disagree   3. A good rule is to use all capital letters so you avoid having to make a decision of whether to capitalize or not.

Agree Disagree   4. All initial letters in a title should be capitalized–including prepositions and articles.

Agree Disagree   5. Italics replaces underscoring.

Agree Disagree   6. Use words to express numbers that are indefinite or approximate.

Agree Disagree   7. Periods and commas go inside the quotation marks.

Agree Disagree   8. Spell checkers on computer programs find all typos, thus eliminating the need for you to check your work.

Agree Disagree   9. Never divide words at the end of the line.

Agree Disagree   10. You can divide a word containing a hyphen at the hyphen.

1. disagree
2. agree
3. disagree
4. disagree
5. agree
6. agree
7. agree
8. disagree
9. disagree
10. agree

Select the better choice from each of the following:

1. abbreviations or acronyms

    a. ABC
    b. Association for Business Communication

2. capitalization

    a. The boss said, "do it as soon as possible."
    b. The boss said, "Do it as soon as possible."

3. capitalization

    a. Please go to the Air Touch Building.
    b. Please go to the air touch building.

4. numbers

    a. The minutes show five members absent.
    b. The minutes show 5 members absent.

5. numbers

    a. She spent $55 and $98.30.
    b. She spent $55.00 and $98.30.

6. punctuation

    a. Susans' report is missing.
    b. Susan's report is missing.

7. punctuation

    a. She was absent from the meeting–not late.
    b. She was–absent from the meeting–not late.

8. punctuation

    a. She said, "The work is fantastic"!
    b. She said, "The work is fantastic!"

9. spelling

    a. Its time to have a meeting.
    b. It's time to have a meeting.

10. word division

    a. specu-lation
    b. spec-ulation

1. b
2. b
3. a
4. a
5. b
6. b
7. a
8. b
9. b
10. a

Polishing Your Writing Mechanics

3

The image reflected by your work will influence your readers' reaction. Your report will be regarded as flawed and viewed with skepticism if it contains numerous mechanical writing errors—even if the report has a wealth of technical, scientific, and creative information.

In school, when teachers told you they were interested in the content of a report—not how pretty it looked or how well written it was, they fibbed! They were influenced by these things as much as by the facts and thoughts in the paper. The mechanics of writing represents an extremely important piece of the writing puzzle.

This chapter cannot possibly cover all there is to know concerning writing skills. However, the basics as well as many of the more common errors made by writers will be included. Topics included are abbreviations and acronyms, capitalization, italics, numbers, punctuation, spelling, and word division.

This chapter can serve as either a short review of ways in which to polish your writing mechanics or as a reference guide while writing. The material included was selected after analyzing common problems made by graduate and undergraduate students in the author's classes.

Abbreviations and Acronyms

Abbreviations in a business report should be used with caution because they may give an impression of rushing or perhaps not really caring. A few exceptions to this follow.

Abbreviations and acronyms–a word formed from the initials letters of a name–of companies, departments, divisions, organizations, or agencies can save a lot of space in a report. Examples include IBM, OSHA, FBI, and DOS. However, if the readers are not familiar with the abbreviations and acronyms used, they may have trouble comprehending or following the meaning of the report. One helpful rule is to always spell out the name in full *the first time it is used* in a business report. However, a person reading only certain parts of the report may still be confused.

Example: Multimedia Design Center (MDC)

In general, the more formal a report, the more abbreviations should be avoided. The following list illustrates places where abbreviations are commonly used.

- Titles before and after names

  Dr. Smith

  Mr. Jones

  Mrs. Miller

  Ms. Reed

  Drs. Forman and Smith

  Mssrs. Smith and Young

  Mary Buck, Ph.D.

  John Jones, Ed.D.

  Julie Smith, M.D.

  Jim Scott, Sr.

- Number when used with a figure   *No. 24*
- Companies and organizations with abbreviations used in letterhead   *Brian & Co.*

- Common abbreviations

  c.o.d.

  6 a.m. and 10 p.m.

  R.S.V.P.

Capitalization

A common dilemma is deciding when to capitalize letters and when to use lowercase letters. This dilemma may be one of the reasons why many people tend to use all capital letters–thus, avoiding the decision entirely. A passage in all uppercase letters is hard to read and, therefore, should be avoided.

These guidelines will provide a foundation for determining what to capitalize. Capitalize the first letter of:

- The first word of a sentence

  Capitalize the first letter of the first word in a sentence.

- The first word of a direct quotation

  The leader said, "Go do your work."

- The first word following a colon

  Do yourself a favor: Practice your writing.

- The names of specific things such as

– people	*Roger Anderson*
– titles of people	*Aunt Donna*
(but not without the name—my aunt)	
– president and vice president of the United States	*the President*
– days and months	*Sunday*
	March
– holidays	*Thanksgiving*
– geographic places	*France*
	Middle East
– buildings, rooms, lakes, rivers, and mountains	*Business Building* *Mono Lake*
– sections of the country	*the West*
(but not directions)	*west*
– nationalities and races	*German*

– languages	*English*
– ships, airplanes, and space vehicles	*Santa Maria* *Discoverer*
– publications	*Newsweek*
– books and articles	*How to Create High Impact Presentations*

      (except for articles–a, an)

      (except for prepositions–of, to, in, on, for, etc.)

      (except for conjunctions–and, but, or, nor, etc.)

– artistic works	*Mona Lisa*
– epithets	*the Big Apple*
– registered trademarks	*Xerox* *Kleenex*
– pronoun I	*I*
– abbreviations	*M.B.A.*
– acronyms	*ADA*

Italics

The use of underscoring in the days of the typewriter was to show material to be italicized when set in type. With the computer, you can eliminate the use of the underscore and replace it with italics.

Italics are useful to:

- Indicate names of books, magazines, newspapers, plays, and movies.

    – *How to Create High-Impact Business Reports* will help you to prepare reports.

- Mix foreign words with English words.

    – She said "*buenos dias.*"

- Place emphasis or highlight a word.

    – She was *guilty*.
    – Please *mark* the item rush.

- Refer to a word as a word

  – The word *rush* was not used.

Numbers

Extreme accuracy is important when using numbers in reports. A writer must decide when to use a number as a figure and when to spell it out. A few basic rules to follow are listed.

- Spell out numbers one through ten.

  The report surveys three companies.

- Use figures for larger numbers.

  The report surveys 50 companies.

- Spell out a number used as the first word of a sentence.

  Fifty years ago this company began operations.

- Use figures in a listing when one of the numbers is higher than ten.

  The committee consists of 3 men and 17 women.

- Use figures to express dates without *th* unless the number is before the month.

  February 20, 19—   20th of February

- Use figures to express sums of money.

  $15 million or $15,000,000

- Use figures to express chapter and page numbers.

  Chapter 5, page 7

- Use figures to express decimals, percentage, dimensions, weights, and temperatures.

  .15   15%   15 x 30   15 pounds   80°

- Use words to express numbers that are indefinite or approximate.

  > *The company employs about five thousand people.*
  > *but*
  > *The company employs 4,321 people.*

- Omit the ciphers in even-dollar figures, unless other numbers in the same sentence include cents.

  > *The cost of the report is $15.*
  > *The costs of the reports are $15.00 and $21.50.*

- Use words to represent time when *o'clock* is used but figures with *p.m.* or *a.m.*

  > *eight o'clock*
  > *8 p.m. or 10 a.m.*

- Omit the minutes unless another time is used in the same sentence where they are needed.

  > *8:30 p.m. or 10:00 a.m. or 9:00 to 5:30*

- Use words for names of streets up to and including twelve.

  > *Third Avenue or First Street but 15th Street*

Punctuation

Punctuation used correctly adds clarity to writing; used incorrectly it can confuse or even distort the meaning. The main types of punctuation are the apostrophe, colon, comma, dash, diagonal, ellipsis points, exclamation, hyphen, parentheses, period, question mark, quotation marks, semicolon, and underscore.

A few general guidelines are reviewed for each of these types of punctuation.

’   The apostrophe shows possession. Use before the *s* if singular; use after if plural or if a word ends with *s*.

- *Paul's report*
- *boy's car but boys' car (if two boys own one car)*

’   Indicates omissions in contractions and in dates.

- *Today's my final report.*
- *She can't read the report today.*
- *The company was founded in '53.*

’   Forms the plural of numbers, letters, and words.

- *Mind your p's and q's.*
- *The report was full of or's and nor's.*

:   Use a colon before a list of items or a series of words–whether listed in the sentence or on separate lines.

- *The following people are exempt: John, Robert, Edward, and Tom.*

- *The following people are exempt:*

John	*Edward*
Robert	*Tom*

:   Use a colon when the second clause *explains or clarifies* the first clause.

- *Reports are vital in the world of business: without them, more meetings would be needed.*

,   Use a comma to separate words, phrases, and clauses in a series.

- *Report preparation consists of planning, writing, and editing.*

,   Use a comma between two adjectives.

- *The attractive, efficient report . . .*

, Use a comma to separate two main clauses.

  – *The report is difficult, and the research will require several days.*

, Use a comma to set off introductory phrases.

  – *Frequently, the work requires . . .*

, Use a comma to set off words, phrases, or clauses that interrupt a sentence.

  – *The work, being completed by a committee, is . . .*
  – *She is, in my opinion, a . . .*
  – *The boss, Robert Smith, is . . .*

– Use a dash to show an afterthought or a summation.

  – *Refer to a piece of art before it appears–not after.*
  – *The staff–including clerical workers, managers, and executives–is to . . .*

– Use a dash to indicate a sudden change of thought.

  – *The report was due last week–but remember the workers were sent home when the water pipes broke.*

/ Use a diagonal or slash to mean one of the two in the expression and/or.

  – *Susan and/or Mark will write the report.*

/ Use a diagonal or slash in fractions, with abbreviations, or with discount terms.

  – *6 2/3   c/o   2/10, n/30*

. . . Use an ellipsis to indicate the omission of parts of a quotation. If at the end of a sentence, use four dots–the period at the end of the sentence accounts for the fourth dot.

  – *"The people will arrive . . . after the event."*
  – *"The people will arrive. . . ."*

!   Use an exclamation point to indicate excitement, emotion, or a command.

-   *The end is near!*

( )   Use parentheses to set off nonessential explanatory words, phrases, or sentences–the use is stronger than a comma but not as strong as a dash.

-   *Please show your costs (lines 73–25).*

.   Use a period at the end of a sentence.

-   *The meeting ended.*

.   Use a period in abbreviations and decimals.

-   *Dr.   Blvd.   5.8%*

?   Use a question mark at the end of any sentence asking a question with an answer expected.

-   *When is the report due?*

?   Use a question mark in parentheses to express doubt.

-   *The company was founded in 1980(?).*

" "   Use quotation marks to enclose a direct quotation. Periods and commas go *inside* the quotation marks; colons, dashes, and semicolons go *outside* the quotations marks. Exclamation points and question marks go inside the quotation marks if they are part of the quoted material and outside if they are not.

-   *She said, "The air is bad."*
-   *Did she say, "The air is bad"?*

"   "   Use quotation marks to enclose titles, words, or phrases borrowed from others or used in a special way.

– *The "Multimedia Design Center" is now open.*

– *A "magic" atmosphere was created.*

;   Use a semicolon to join two independent clauses not separated by a coordinating conjunction such as *and, but, or,* or *nor.*

– *The work is completed; the report will be mailed next week.*

;   Use a semicolon to connect two main clauses using a conjunctive adverb such as *however, nevertheless, consequently, therefore, moreover, hence,* and *furthermore.*

– *The work is not completed; however, it will be mailed by the end of the month.*

;   Use a semicolon to clarify series of words and phrases requiring other internal comma punctuation.

– *The executive staff consists of John Johnston, President; Marcia West, Vice-President; Susan Miller, Secretary; and Ron Smith, Treasurer.*

-       Use a hyphen in compound surnames.

– *Rhodes-Hanna*

-       Use a hyphen to separate numbers such as in telephone or social security numbers.

– *(909) 869-1000 or 512-34-5489*

-       Use a hyphen when two adjectives work together to modify a noun.

– *well-written book or first-rate hotel*

-       Use a hyphen in word division at the end of a line when lines fall short or are too long. (See Word Division rules.)

– *profes- sor   or knowl- edge*

   —   Use the underscore to indicate italics (if you are unable to use the italics).

         — *the name of the book is* <u>How to Create High-Impact Business Reports</u>

Spelling

Using correct spelling is important in a business report if you want to create a favorable image. Spelling checkers are available on many word processing and desktop publishing software programs; however, the spelling checkers are unable to pick up some types of errors.

The following list of words illustrates types of errors that would not be found by a spell checker on the computer. You must check a regular dictionary to be sure you have the right word.

accede	*exceed*
accept	*except*
access	*excess*
ad	*add*
adapt	*adept*
addition	*edition*
advice	*advise*
affect	*effect*
all ready	*already*
all ways	*always*
allowed	*aloud*
any way	*anyway*
are	*our, hour*
capital	*capitol*
cease	*sieze*
cite	*sight, site*

complement	*compliment*
council	*counsel*
descent	*dissent*
desert	*dessert*
device	*devise*
disapprove	*disprove*
disburse	*disperse*
dual	*duel*
elicit	*illicit*
emigrate	*immigrate*
develop	*envelope*
expand	*expend*
farther	*further*
foreword	*forward*
formally	*formerly*
forth	*fourth*
incidence	*incidents*
interstate	*intrastate*
its	*it's*
knew	*new*
later	*latter*
leased	*least*
lessen	*lesson*
maybe	*may be*
passed	*past*
personal	*personnel*
principal	*principle*
role	*roll*
stationary	*stationery*
suit	*suite*
than	*then*
their	*there*
to	*too, two*
weak	*week*
weather	*whether*

dual

Which one do I want??

In high-impact business reports, the correctly spelled and selected word can create a favorable reader impression.

duel

Word Division

Dividing words at the end of a line can be another difficult decision. Many word processing and desktop publishing programs include a feature that will allow you to control the word divisions used within your report.

As Chapter 6 will show, you may choose to manually control hyphenation (referred to as force hyphenate). Some of the programs will give you suggestions on acceptable word divisions.

However, you will need to be aware of a few general guidelines in making wise decisions on when, where, and how to divide. A good rule of word division is don't! However, you may find that you must sometimes divide words to make lines end evenly on the right or, if using full justification, to prevent large spaces between words. You may even find, on occasion, that to have proper line endings you need to rewrite, rearrange, or restate your thought. If you must divide words, use the following guidelines.

- Avoid dividing in the first and last lines of a paragraph or a page.

- Avoid dividing in more than two lines in a row.

- Divide only between syllables–thus, one-syllable words cannot be divided.

- Keep a single-vowel syllable with the first part of the word.

    (such as form-ulation)   *suggest formu-lation*

- Do not divide a word of five or fewer letters.

    cable   ideal   into   icon

- Do not divide a word if only two letters will appear on the next line.

  (such as in careful-ly)   *suggest care-fully*

- Do not divide a word if only one letter is left on the first line.

  (such as in a-board)   *suggest no division*

- Divide compound words between the two words.

  sales-person   *desk-top*

- Divide words containing a hyphen at the hyphen.

  self-evident   *twenty-three*

The Bottom Line

The mechanics of writing involve many different topics. Rather than memorizing all the rules, you may find it better to keep a good reference manual handy. This chapter can be used as a review as well as serving as a quick reference to basic writing mechanics.

In the next chapter, you will become acquainted with how to give credit where credit is due. The difference between honesty and plagiarism may be a simple reference.

Diagnostic Glimpse #4

How do you give proper credit to your resources?

How carefully do you need to read Chapter 4, "Crediting Your Resources"? The questions below will help you discover how much you already know about types of resources, methods of quoting, citing sources, and style manuals.

Agree   Disagree   1. Giving credit to others takes away from your work.

Agree   Disagree   2. Primary sources consist of information found in books, periodicals, and other publications.

Agree   Disagree   3. Direct quotations may appear to be more authoritative.

Agree   Disagree   4. A direct quotation of five lines or 40 words should be enclosed with quotation marks.

Agree   Disagree   5. Paraphrasing passages may tie cited works in better with your writing and also take less space.

Agree   Disagree   6. Although the use of footnotes may be more convenient for the reader, the report may be more difficult to produce.

Agree   Disagree   7. Endnotes have a major advantage when papers are to be microfilmed.

Agree   Disagree   8. Parenthetical references provide the advantages of both footnotes and endnotes.

Agree   Disagree   9. In a parenthetical reference, the last name of the author is separated from the date by a comma.

Agree   Disagree   10. Reference style manuals should be used for more formal reports.

10. agree
9. agree
8. agree
7. disagree
6. agree
5. agree
4. disagree
3. agree
2. disagree
1. disagree

Name the two types of resources used in references.

secondary
primary

Identify two methods of quoting.

paraphrasing
direct

List three methods for citing sources.

parenthetical references
endnotes
footnotes

Name five popular style manuals.

(abbreviated)
A Manual for Writers
MLA
Chicago Manual
Form and Style
APA

Reference this book using one of the above style manual formats.

A Manual for Writers
MLA
Chicago Manual
Form and Style

Lincolnwood, Illinois: NTC Publishing Group, 1995.
Kupsh, Joyce. *How to Create High-Impact Business Reports*.
APA

Lincolnwood, Illinois: NTC Publishing Group.
Kupsh, J. (1995). *How to create high-impact business reports*.

Crediting Your Resources

Credit should be given where credit is due! For legal, ethical, and moral reasons, you need to credit any secondary resources in your work. Giving credit to others does not take away but actually lends support and authority to your work. Fiction and personal experiences are the only types of writing where references are not needed.

Types of Resources

Resources may be either primary or secondary. According to their use, the difference in these two types is subject to interpretation.

Primary

Primary sources are original materials such as surveys, interviews, letters, diaries, etc. In general, any material that has not been analyzed or interpreted.

Secondary

In contrast, secondary sources consist of information found in books, periodicals, and other publications. Such writings are considered information that includes an interpretation by the author. Although some writers may want to separate the primary and

Crediting your resources is a way of being honest while lending credibility to your work. In authoring a novel, you are creating fiction. In writing business reports, you are creatively using resources–both secondary and original–to provide the facts and to justify your position.

secondary sources in a bibliography, the referencing techniques are the same.

Methods of Quoting

Secondary sources may be used in one of two ways. They may be quoted directly or they may be paraphrased–put in your own words. A writer has the flexibility of choosing either one; however, making use of both at different places in your report may be the best solution.

Direct Quotations

A direct quotation assures your readers that you have not changed the meaning. In addition, it may also appear to be more authoritative. The fact that you are quoting information should be made obvious to the reader. Direct quotations of five lines or more than 40 words should be blocked and indented or set in from both margins by approximately five spaces or one-half an inch. When this is done, quotation marks are not used at the beginning or the end, though they may be necessary for some internal passages.

Also, the insertion of personal comments and the indication of an omission are both possible in direct quotations. In a quotation, you may insert your comments between brackets. One inclusion commonly used is the Latin word *sic*. The word is not an abbreviation, so no period should be used. The term means *so, thus,* or *in this manner* and is used to show a misspelling or a grammatical error in the original quotation.

Omissions are made by using ellipsis points–a series of three periods (...). If the ellipsis occurs at the end of the sentence, you need to use an additional point for the ending of the sentence–or four periods (see Chapter 3–"Polishing Your Writing Mechanics").

As previously noted, a quotation of less than five lines or 40 words can be included in the text using quotation marks to distinguish it from your writing. If a direct quotation is more than a page or so in length, be sure to select only the most relevant portion. Or, you may want to simply refer to it in the text of the report and include it as an appendix. Conversely, anything included in the appendix should be mentioned in the report at the appropriate place.

Paraphrasing

Restating material in your own words as an indirect quotation is called paraphrasing. Paraphrasing passages rather than directly quoting passages may tie the work in better with your writing and also take less space.

Even though quotation marks are not used, a reader should always be able to tell exactly what is paraphrased and what is your own work. Ways of accomplishing this goal are statements such as:

> *According to Xxx, . . .*
> *Xxx states that . . .*
> *Xxx found that . . .*

Citing Sources

A variety of methods for citing sources is available. Three general methods are (1) footnotes, (2) endnotes, and (3) parenthetical references.

Each of these methods has a place, but a brief parenthetical reference in the text with a complete listing of the source at the end of either a section or the report is perhaps the most popular choice today. This method is probably the easiest and also the most convenient for the reader.

Footnotes

Footnotes are made by placing a raised number in the text at the end of the quotation–either direct or paraphrased. Identification is then placed at the bottom of the page under a 1-inch line.

¹Kupsh and Graves, p.38

The first time a reference appears, a complete listing is used. Subsequent references to the same work should have a shortened version. Latin abbreviations–*ibid., op. cit.,* and *loc. cit.*– tend to be confusing and are no longer recommended.

Even though footnotes may be convenient for the reader, they often make the production of the report much more difficult. Extensive planning is needed to be sure that the footnote appears on the page where it was used and that proper spacing is left at the bottom of the page. In addition to the footnote, a complete listing of sources also needs to be included at the end of the section, chapter, or report.

Endnotes

Endnotes are indicated in the text by a raised number, though some systems may use a number in parenthesis on the same line as the text. The endnote eliminates the need for footnotes at the bottom of the page. Instead, a complete listing of the sources in numerical order is included at the end of the report along with an alphabetized list of those same references. This method requires two lists but eliminates the tedious task of placing footnotes at the bottom of a page.

A major disadvantage of this reference style occurs in papers that are to be microfilmed–such as theses and dissertations. A reader using microfilm must flip back and forth to identify the source of a quotation.

(Kupsh and Graves, p.52)

Parenthetical Reference

In parenthetical references, a shortened reference is placed in parentheses within the text. A complete listing of these sources is then placed at the end of the section, chapter, or report.

Parenthetical references provide the advantages of both footnotes and endnotes. They are easy for the writer to use and they provide adequate, convenient information for the reader.

For these reasons, this style is the one chosen for the sample report in Appendix B. The sample gives important information on how to write a report but also serves as an example.

In using parenthetical references, place the last name of the author and the date in parentheses–separated by a comma. The name of a corporation, the name of a work, or some other means of identification may also be used with the date.

If the author's name is mentioned in the text, then you need use only the date in parentheses. If you refer to both the author and the date in the text, nothing needs to be put in parentheses; however, the reference will still be included in the alphabetical listing at the end. If the quote is from a specific page, ideally you should include the page number in case a reader wants to locate the original writing.

Style Manuals

Numerous reference styles are available depending upon your need. A more formal style is needed for collegiate writing–such as a thesis or dissertation, while a less technical approach is probably adequate for business needs.

Popular style guides or manuals are (1) *Publication Manual of the American Psychological Association* (APA), (2) *Form and Style: Research Papers, Reports, and Theses* by Slade, Campbell, and Ballou, (3) *The Chicago Manual of Style*, (4) *MLA Handbook for Writers of Research Papers* by Gibaldi and Achtert, and (5) *A Manual for Writers of Term Papers, Theses and Dissertations* by Turabian. Examples of citing sources for a book, a magazine article, a journal article, a newspaper, an unpublished document, and a speech are given according to each of these style manuals in the following boxes.

If you have other types of material to reference, try to establish some logical arrangement by following the examples provided. Remember to use common sense and to be consistent.

Publication Manual of the American Psychological Association

Book

American Psychological Association. (1994). *Publication manual of the American Psychological Association* (4th ed.). Washington, DC: Author.

Book

Kupsh, J. (1995). *How to create high-impact business reports.* Lincolnwood, Illinois: NTC Publishing Group.

Magazine

Mello, A. (1994, April). Upgrading to PowerPC: Mapping a route to new Macs. *Macworld*, pp. 21–22.

Journal

Altbach, P. G., & Lewis, L. (1994, Winter). Reforming higher education: A modest proposal. *The NEA Higher Education Journal, 9* (2), 31–40.

Newspaper

Groves, M. (1994, February 4). Memo pads give way to modems. *Los Angeles Times,* pp. 1, 26–27.

Unpublished Paper

Carter, K. D. (1992). *A study of the impact of the graduate course professional presentations using technology.* Unpublished master's thesis, California State Polytechnic University, Pomona.

Speech

Kupsh, J., & Buck, M. (1994, April). *Developing computer-based and multimedia presentations.* Presentation at the annual meeting of Association for Business Communication West Regional Conference, Redondo Beach, CA.

Form and Style: Research Papers, Reports, and Theses

Slade, Carole C., William Campbell, and Stephen Ballou. *Form and Style: Research Papers, Reports, and Theses.* 8th ed. Boston: Houghton Mifflin Company, 1994.

Book

Kupsh, Joyce. *How to Create High-Impact Business Reports.* Lincolnwood, Illinois: NTC Publishing Group, 1995.

Book

Mello, Adrian. "Upgrading to PowerPC: Mapping a Route to New Macs." *Macworld*, April 1994: 21–22.

Magazine

Altbach, Philip G., and Lionel S. Lewis. "Reforming Higher Education: A Modest Proposal." *The NEA Higher Education Journal* 9, no. 2 (1994): 31–40.

Journal

Groves, Martha. "Memo Pads Give Way to Modems." *Los Angeles Times,* 4 February 1994: Business 1, 26–27.

Newspaper

Carter, Kristin Dee. "A Study of the Impact of the Graduate Course Professional Presentations Using Technology." Unpublished master's thesis, California State Polytechnic University, Pomona, 1992.

Unpublished Paper

Kupsh, Joyce, and Mary Buck. *Developing Computer-Based and Multimedia Presentations.* Presentation at the annual meeting of Association for Business Communication West Regional Conference, Redondo Beach, California, 15 April 1994.

Speech

The Chicago Manual of Style

Book

The Chicago Manual of Style. 14th ed. Chicago: University of Chicago Press, 1993.

Book

Kupsh, Joyce. *How to Create High-Impact Business Reports*. Lincolnwood, Illinois: NTC Publishing Group, 1995.

Magazine

Mello, Adrian. "Upgrading to PowerPC: Mapping a Route to New Macs." *Macworld*, April 1994, 21–22.

Journal

Altbach, Philip G., and Lionel S. Lewis. "Reforming Higher Education: A Modest Proposal." *The NEA Higher Education Journal* 9, no. 2 (April 1994): 31–40.

Newspaper

Groves, Martha. "Memo Pads Give Way to Modems." *Los Angeles Times*, 4 February 1994, 1, 26–27.

Unpublished Paper

Carter, Kristin Dee. "A Study of the Impact of the Graduate Course Professional Presentations Using Technology." MBA thesis, California State Polytechnic University, Pomona, 1992.

Speech

Kupsh, Joyce, and Mary Buck. "Developing Computer-Based and Multimedia Presentations." Presentation at the annual meeting of Association for Business Communication West Regional Conference. Redondo Beach, California, 15 April 1994.

MLA Handbook
for Writers of Research Papers

Gibaldi, Joseph, and Walter S. Achtert. *MLA Handbook for Writers of Research Papers.* 3rd ed. New York: Modern Language Association, 1988.

Book

Kupsh, Joyce. *How to Create High-Impact Business Reports.* Lincolnwood, Illinois: NTC Publishing Group, 1995.

Book

Mello, Adrian. "Upgrading to PowerPC: Mapping a route to new Macs." *Macworld*, April 1994: 21–22.

Magazine

Altbach, Philip G., and Lionel S. Lewis. "Reforming Higher Education: A Modest Proposal." *The NEA Higher Education Journal*, 9.2 (1994): 31–40.

Journal

Groves, Martha. "Memo Pads Give Way to Modems." *Los Angeles Times,* 4 February 1994: Business 1, 26–27.

Newspaper

Carter, Kristin Dee. "A Study of the Impact of the Graduate Course Professional Presentations Using Technology." Unpublished master's thesis, California State Polytechnic University, Pomona, 1992.

Unpublished Paper

Kupsh, Joyce, and Mary Buck. "Developing Computer-Based and Multimedia Presentations." Presentation at the annual meeting of Association for Business Communication West Regional Conference, Redondo Beach, California, 15 April 1994.

Speech

A Manual for Writers of Term Papers, Theses and Dissertations

Book

Turabian, Kate L. *A Manual for Writers of Term Papers, Theses and Dissertations.* Chicago: University of Chicago Press, 1987.

Book

Kupsh, Joyce. *How to Create High-Impact Business Reports.* Lincolnwood, Illinois: NTC Publishing Group, 1995.

Magazine

Mello, Adrian. "Upgrading to PowerPC: Mapping a Route to New Macs." *Macworld*, (April 1994), 21–22.

Journal

Altbach, Philip G., and Lionel S. Lewis. "Reforming Higher Education: A Modest Proposal." *The NEA Higher Education Journal*, IX, No. 2 (Winter 1994), 31–40.

Newspaper

Groves, Martha. "Memo Pads Give Way to Modems." *Los Angeles Times,* (February 4, 1994), Business 1, 26–27.

Unpublished Paper

Carter, Kristin Dee. "A Study of the Impact of the Graduate Course Professional Presentations Using Technology." Unpublished Master's thesis, California State Polytechnic University, Pomona, 1992.

Speech

Kupsh, Joyce, and Mary Buck. "Developing Computer-Based and Multimedia Presentations." Presentation at the annual meeting of Association for Business Communication West Regional Conference, Redondo Beach, California, April 15, 1994.

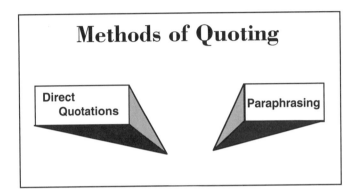

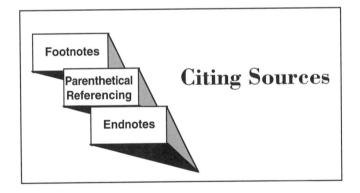

Be Legal!

      Be Ethical!

            Show Credibility!

The Bottom Line

Crediting resources in your writing is not only ethical and legal but also lends creditability to your report. Documentation is a way of showing support for your ideas–thus, making your work more authoritative. Citing references also keeps you honest.

Numerous style manuals are available for you to follow. If you are writing a thesis, a dissertation, or an article for a scientific publication, you should obtain and use the requested style format. However, if you are writing a business report, the examples in this chapter can be used as guidelines.

The next chapter helps you to determine the type of format for your report. In addition, it examines the classifications of reports and reviews the various elements that can be included to make a report more effective.

Diagnostic Glimpse #5

Are you aware of the various formats and forms available for a report?

How carefully do you need to read Chapter 5, "Looking at Format and Form"? The questions below will help you discover how much you already know about report classifications, format choices, and the parts of a report.

Agree   Disagree   1.   The general look of reports should not be changed from the traditional look of reports made over the years.

Agree   Disagree   2.   The reason for writing a report is generally to inform, interpret, recommend, persuade, or some combination of these reasons.

Agree   Disagree   3.   A good format gets attention and makes reading easier.

Agree   Disagree   4.   Report formats can be a memo or letter.

Agree   Disagree   5.   If a form is required for a report, you must use a typewriter.

Agree   Disagree   6.   The best format for a report is always to use 8 1/2 x 11 paper with a 1-inch left margin and a 1-inch right margin.

Agree   Disagree   7.   A newsletter is a printed report providing news to a special group.

Agree   Disagree   8.   Brochures may be an effective way of making a report.

Agree   Disagree   9.   The parts of a report will vary according to its specific aims and purposes.

Agree   Disagree   10.   A cover letter or memo is not necessary if the report states the purpose.

1. disagree
2. agree
3. agree
4. agree
5. disagree
6. disagree
7. agree
8. agree
9. agree
10. disagree

Give four different classifications of reasons for writing a report.

inform
interpret
recommend
persuade

Name at least six different choices in formatting a report.

memo or letter
form
traditional
manuscript
newsletter
brochure
magazine, booklet,
or manual

List nine different parts of a report that you may want to consider including.

title page
table of contents
executive summary
or abstract
body
appendices
bibliography/ref-
erences/resources
glossary
index
cover memo/letter

Looking at Format and Form

B usiness reports of today do not have to look like the traditional reports of yesterday. You can now take advantage of the various design elements and techniques provided by desktop publishing technology. A wide variety of formats are available.

A report is typically an account of balances or a presentation of detailed information. It can relate to business, technical, or sales/marketing proposals and reflect daily, weekly, monthly, or annual data. It can certainly be made to look more interesting than the boring 10- or 50-page papers that were frequently the assignment given to you in school. A report does not have to look like a report. It can look interesting and make you want to read it!

Classifications of Reports

All reports are written for a reason. The reason may be to inform, interpret, recommend, persuade, or some combination of the same.

Inform

Reports to inform may tell of status or progress and may include financial facts. Examples of reports falling into this classification are:

- A company's annual report

Chapter 1 shared many ideas of how you can use new technology to design your report. These desktop publishing techniques can be used in many different ways. The format of your report is important in ensuring that it will receive favorable notice and attention. This chapter will also discuss different elements a report can have to make it more effective.

- The status of sales performance for a week/month/quarter/year

- An update on the progress of your new company headquarters under construction

- Procedures to be followed–such as for a move to the new building site

- Minutes of a meeting

- Documentation of occurrences or events–such as a conversation or an accident

- Financial reports–such as credit reports, income statement/balance sheet showing financial position, etc.

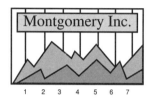

Interpret

Rather than simply stating the condition, interpretive reports advance to a higher level, going beyond the facts and including an analysis or interpretation of the facts. Examples of this type of report are:

- Sales or marketing reports analyzing the reasons for an increase or decrease in a given period of time

- Research and development reports analyzing the performance standards of a new product

- Scientific or technical reports investigating numerous activities

- Financial reports explaining the budget needs for a new venture

Recommend

Reports may include information and provide an interpretive analysis and then also go to the next step of providing solutions or recommendations. Any of

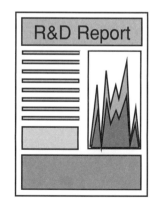

the reports listed under the previous category may include a recommendation. Other examples are:

- Theses or dissertations investigating a topic, conducting original research–such as a survey, a series of interviews, an experimental study– analyzing the results, and providing recommendations for the future

- Investigation and analysis of a product or company with recommendations of how improvements can be made

Persuade

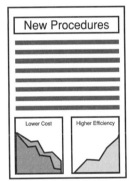

Reports may be written in an attempt to persuade or generate action of some type. A persuasive report may contain elements of all three previous types of reports–inform, interpret, and recommend–but then go one step more and add an emotional appeal to the recommendation. Examples are:

- Sales proposals soliciting new business from clients

- Requests for a change of some type

- Solicitation of funds for a given task or activity

Format Choices

Format choices for any of the various classifications of reports will be examined next. All reports should be attractively produced in an easy-to-read format, but the need may be even greater if a report is to recommend or persuade. The facts and figures in the report are of no value if the intended audience never reads it.

The value of a good format is that it gets the attention of the receiver and makes the task of reading easy. Formats for a report include a memo or letter, a form, the traditional manuscript with variations, a newsletter, a brochure, and a magazine, booklet, or manual.

Memo or Letter

Many information reports need be nothing more than a memo. The memo heading can be the company stationery provided for memos. Such stationery is intended for use in communicating with people within the office or company. In contrast, letterhead stationery is normally used if correspondence is with someone outside of the company.

By creating a personalized template, you can create your own memo heading. Advantages of creating a template of your own can be twofold: (1) you will not need to rekey your own identification information each time you write a memo, and (2) you can use a design including clip art that is different and therefore attracts favorable notice.

Using either memo or letterhead stationery may be the appropriate vehicle for many of your reports. If the reports are longer than two or three pages, however, you may find it better to use the memo or letterhead stationery only for a cover message. This cover message could be kept short but is effective in introducing or explaining the attached or enclosed report.

If the contents of the report can be included in a short memo or letter, you can still take advantage of the desktop publishing features suggested in Chapter 6–"Designing Your Document." For instance, side-headings using bold and larger font sizes and graphics and art can still be used. Such devices make the information more attractive resulting in easier reading or scanning.

Form

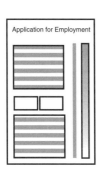

Many times a report is made by completing a form. If the form is in a digitized format, you have the advantage of being able to key in the requested information.

If you are unable to get a digitized copy of the form, check and see if you have access to a scanner with OCR (optical character recognition) software capable of reading the form into your computer. This process is helpful even if you may have to perform some cleanup work after it is digitized. Scanning is rarely performed with 100 percent accuracy.

When electronic scanning is not an option, you may want to take the time to replicate the form (or if you are lucky, have someone else do it) by keying it into your computer. Even though this task is time-consuming, it may be worth the effort–particularly if reporting on the same form is going to be needed again in the future.

Otherwise, you are stuck with the task of finding an old-fashioned typewriter and going back to the days of trying to align the type and make the corrections. Or, the last option may be to complete the report in longhand. Neither of these options will show off your information to the best advantage. If only factual information is required and you are not attempting to win an important proposal, get attention, or impress the audience, these options may adequately meet the needs in a time-efficient manner. However, many times your needs will be more than just reporting the data. If your report is longer than a page or two or the report is to recommend or persuade, you should consider other types of formats.

Traditional Manuscript

A traditional paper does not have to look like a traditional manuscript. By applying the desktop publishing techniques discussed in Chapter 6, a manuscript can look like a magazine article or an annual company report.

Depending upon the binding requirements (see Chapter 7), the margins can be 1 inch on each side (or 1 1/4 or 1 1/2 inches allowing for binding needs). Yet, by using several levels of subheadings, a variety of font sizes and styles, and graphics and art, the finished product is suddenly a professional-looking business report rather than yesterday's style.

One variation is to allow more space on either the right or left side for headings and subheadings, side notes, and illustrations. The advantage of this technique is readability. Also, white space is available for the reader to scribble notes or make additions or corrections if desired. This book uses such a format.

Newsletter

The goal of a newsletter is to communicate information to readers. A typical newsletter is a printed report providing news to a special group.

The special group may be people within an organization; the newsletter then becomes a communication device allowing information to flow either upward to management or downward to the

employees. The special interest group may be individuals outside of a company who are concerned with a special topic–such as members of a professional organization or a hobby club.

Newsletters may be information reports that are published on a timely basis–such as monthly, quarterly, or yearly. A challenge in designing a newsletter is to develop a format and general identifying look but to make each particular newsletter unique.

A newsletter may range in length from 1 to 20 pages and use either standard- or legal-size paper. Frequently, newsletters are made with double-size paper and folded on the left but can also be bound together by being stapled at the fold or stapled in the left-hand corner.

Ideas to keep in mind in producing a newsletter are:

FLY AIRLINES

- Develop a logotype, nameplate, or flag for the title–usually on the first sheet either at the top or left edge

- Create a masthead listing the editor(s) and any others responsible for the publication along with their addresses, phone numbers, etc.

- Establish a volume, number, date, etc., if the publication is to be an ongoing one

- Choose desired column and type sizes–if narrower columns, use a smaller type size

- Keep text readable–usually defined as seven to ten words on each line

- Add interest with graphics and art–a good idea is to break monotony by using text wrap techniques around the art

- Use top and bottom rules to set off the page boundaries

- Use column gutter rules to allow for a visual break

- Choose a thickness for rules that does not overpower or get lost

- Consider allowing space for applying a label and sending as a self-mailer without an envelope

Brochure

A brochure is a flyer, leaflet, or small pamphlet and is used in almost every area of business and education. A common use of a brochure is an announcement appropriate for advertising a meeting or a product. However, it can also be used for a fairly brief informative report.

A well-done brochure presents a lot of information in an attractive manner. For example, a brochure may contain an announcement of a product or a meeting, education material, or a persuasive message.

Information on a brochure can be printed on both sides of a sheet of paper. Although the paper can be any size, standard 8 1/2 x 11 paper or legal 8 1/2 x 14 paper are the most frequent choices. Either a vertical or horizontal orientation is possible. A few tips to keep in mind when preparing brochures are:

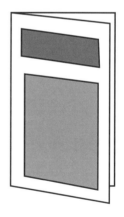

Double-fold
Brochure

- Be sure the information is complete–when, where, why, who, and how

- Break the information into panels–for instance, a tri-fold on standard paper will have six different panels

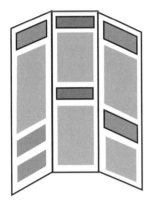

Tri-fold Brochure

- Draft a sample *dummy* to see how the finished project will look

- Keep the information simple

- Include appropriate graphics and visuals to make the brochure attention-getting

- Select a small font size for the body text and vary the font sizes on other text to make the important information stand out

- Turn some of the information into bullet listings or enumerations rather than using regular paragraphs

- Use one of the panels to make the flyer into a self-mailer so that an envelope is not needed

- Purchase color designed paper and plan the brochure around the design on the paper

- Purchase brochures with a built-in perforated business card that can be torn out by the reader

Magazine, Booklet, or Manual

The main difference between a newsletter or brochure and a magazine, booklet, or manual is that the latter contain more pages. *Magazine, booklet,* or *manual* are terms used somewhat interchangeably and could be considered in the book category. In fact, the techniques mentioned under "newsletters" also apply in this category; however, the page size will probably be reduced to standard sizes (see "Layout and Design" in Chapter 6).

Parts of a Report

The parts of a report will vary according to its specific aims and purposes. This section will provide an overview of all the various parts that can be included along with an explanation of when and why the various parts should be used.

Title Page

A title page provides identification and should include information such as:

- Title of report
- Author or authors of report–and possibly company, address, phone number of the author(s)
- Date of report
- Purpose of report–prepared for whom and why

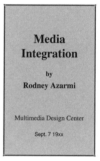

Executive Summary/Abstract

An executive summary or abstract of the report states in approximately a page a synopsis of the entire report. In the business world, an executive summary is extremely important. The executive summary may be read and used to judge whether the report is worth reading. On the other hand, the executive summary may be effective in helping the reader to make a favorable decision without reading the rest of the report. *Consider your report successful if this happens! Possibly because of its overall look of attractiveness and efficiency, your report portrays a confidence that leads to acceptance.*

The executive summary or abstract should state the report in a nutshell–generally, it could include the purpose or objectives of the report, background, procedures or approach to the report, findings, and summary, recommendations, and conclusions (if any).

Table of Contents

Because *Table of Contents* is somewhat redundant, a Table of Contents can also be referred to simply as *Contents*. Any report more than three or four pages long can benefit from the inclusion of such a page. Thus, the formats of memos, letters, or forms would not need one.

The elements of this page should include *Contents* or *Table of Contents* at the top along with the headings and subheadings and the page numbers where they appear. Worded another way, the contents page is an outline; however, Roman and Arabic numbers used in the typical outline should not be included unless they are used in the report. Typically, a report uses numbers only on sections or chapters. A reference manual may include a more detailed numbering system to help in locating a specific section.

Leaders or dots are used to help the reader follow the text over to the page numbers. Most word processing or desktop publishing programs have an automatic way of inserting the leaders. Some programs even include a way of automatically generating the contents page by flagging the sections during the keyboarding process.

A contents page may include all levels of headings or may be restricted to only one or two levels. In making this decision and developing a contents page, the purposes of such a page should be remembered–to provide an overview of what the report includes and to allow readers to locate and read only certain sections.

Body

The body may contain a variety of different parts to fit various situations. The generic outline presented below probably sounds similar to a term paper or thesis assignment from school, but it provides some useful guidelines for any report.

Introduction
Related Research
Procedures or Methodology
Findings
Summary, Recommendations, and Conclusions

Appendices

An appendix (singular) or appendices (plural) contains supporting material to the report. The plural form can also be spelled *appendixes*. This supporting material may include longer information that may be needed for verification or backup information but might distract from the normal reading flow. Examples are listings, statistics, quotations, etc. Items in an appendix should be referred to at the appropriate place in the report as Appendix A, Appendix B, etc. and placed in the order that they were mentioned.

Bibliography/References/Resources

Although frequently used interchangeably, bibliographies, references, and resources are not exactly the same thing. A bibliography contains a list of writings on a subject. References are used to list citings made. Resources indicates where additional information on a subject can be found.

Glossary

A glossary contains a list of specialized words or terms with their meanings. A glossary is normally found at the end of the report. In very technical reports, however, you might want to include terminology needed for the report in the introduction section of the report.

Index

An index is used in longer reports, manuals, or books to help readers find the page of a specific topic. Some word processing and desktop publishing programs are able to generate an index in two different ways.

One method is to flag all words in the text that should be included in the index. In the second method, you key in a list of words to be included in the index and let the computer search and make you a list of page numbers where each of the words appears. This capability can save hours of tedious searching in addition to being more accurate.

Cover Memo/Letter

A cover memo (if inside your organization) or letter of transmittal (if outside your organization) is frequently advised to let the receiver(s) know what they are receiving and why. This correspondence may also highlight and give the findings or conclusions of the report. Similar to the executive summary, a direct approach in letting the reader(s) know the ending is advisable in the busy world of business. In a novel, the ending should be saved for the end. In the business world, you may have an exciting ending that when stated at the beginning will entice the reader(s) to read or scan the report.

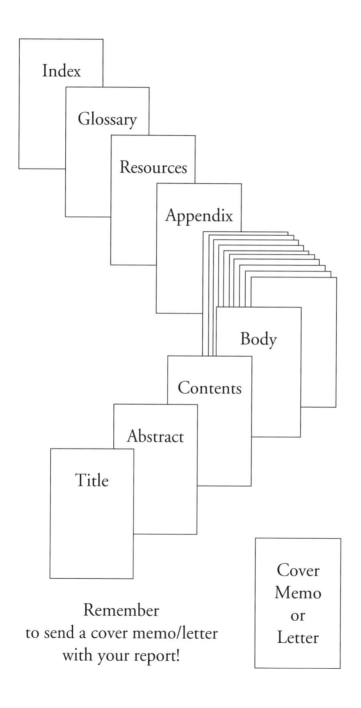

Index

Glossary

Resources

Appendix

Body

Contents

Abstract

Title

Remember
to send a cover memo/letter
with your report!

Cover
Memo
or
Letter

The Bottom Line

Determining what format to use is an important step in creating a high impact report. By being aware of the various classifications of reports, the types of formats possible for reports, and the typical parts of a report, you can decide what is appropriate for your individual needs.

Remember, however, that a report is similar to a car. An attractive look and style can draw interest, but you normally want to test drive a car before you buy. If you open up the hood and find no engine or a defective one, you are not going to buy the car–even though the car looks pretty. On a similar basis, a report must have something inside.

Word processing and desktop publishing features can give your reports a new look. Chapter 6 examines how to use these new features in designing your document.

Read this Diagnostic Glimpse before Chapter 6.

Diagnostic Glimpse #6

How familiar are you with the desktop publishing techniques and tools available with today's computers?

How carefully do you need to read Chapter 6, "Designing Your Document"? The questions below will help you discover how much you already know about typography, layout and design, graphics and art, and color.

Agree   Disagree   1. Professional typesetters and graphic artists are required for producing a professional-looking report.

Agree   Disagree   2. Word processing and desktop publishing overlap and tend to be used interchangeably.

Agree   Disagree   3. The main elements of designing a document are typography, layout and design, graphics and art, and color.

Agree   Disagree   4. A variety of typefaces and fonts are available for microcomputer users in preparing their reports.

Agree   Disagree   5. All capital or uppercase letters makes a visual easier to read.

Agree   Disagree   6. A two-column format is not appropriate for a report.

Agree   Disagree   7. Either a portrait or landscape orientation may be effective for a report.

Agree   Disagree   8. Headings and subheadings are not essential in a report.

Agree   Disagree   9. When utilizing a double-page layout, you should use even numbers on the right-hand facing page.

Agree   Disagree   10. Using graphics in a report is possible on many desktop computers of today.

1. disagree
2. agree
3. agree
4. agree
5. disagree
6. disagree
7. agree
8. disagree
9. disagree
10. agree

1. The bottom of the main part of a letter is called _____.

2. A kind of type without the small cross strokes or flares at the ends of a letter's main stems, providing a cleaner, simpler look, is referred to as _____ type.

3. Type size is measured by using the typesetters terms' of _____ and _____.

4. The logical size for text body ranges from __ to __ points.

5. The space between lines is called line spacing or _____.

6. The term _____ refers to overall spacing within a group of letters, a word, or a line or more of text.

7. The type of alignment in which both the left and the right margins are flush is called _____.

8. The space between the two columns in a two-columnar format is referred to as the _____.

9. To help readers locate a particular section or area within a report, you should use either _____ or _____.

10. Visual elements such as photographs, drawings, graphs, charts, icons, lines, boxes, patterns, and background tints may be referred to as _____.

11. Copyright-free art created by someone else for you to paste into your document is called _____.

12. The price of having color printers connected to a computer is rapidly _____ .

13. In the printing process, the process of making negatives for the four plates is called a _____ process, which uses three colors plus black.

14. Preprinted color designed _____ is available from companies such as Paper Direct, Inc. to enhance your reports.

15. Unless full-color photographs are used, you should usually limit the use of color to _____ or _____ colors.

---

1. baseline
2. sans serif
3. points and picas
4. 8 to 12
5. leading
6. tracking
7. justification
8. gutter
9. headers or footers
10. graphics
11. clip art
12. decreasing
13. subtractive
14. paper
15. 3 or 4 colors

Designing Your Document

No longer do your reports have to look like diaries or essays. Instead, they can look like professional publications. Today's technology makes it possible for you to create–on your desktop with your computer and laser printer–daily reports using the high-quality typesetting formerly associated only with such things as the annual report.

Specialists such as typesetters, graphic artists, designers, copy editors, and professional press people are still around and can serve a major role in the final production of written materials. However, writers of today are probably using equipment capable of producing attractive, eye-catching results without the need of such experts–resulting in high-impact reports at comparatively low cost. This process is called desktop publishing.

Desktop publishing is defined by Que's *Computer User's Dictionary* (1990) as:

> The use of a personal computer system as an inexpensive production system for generating typeset-quality text and graphics. Desktop publishers often merge text and graphics on the same page and print pages on a high-resolution laser printer or typesetting machine.

This definition does not specifically say or require that desktop publishing software be used. Originally, word processing software was intended for

From this chapter, you will obtain the basics needed to turn your documents into reports that will be eye-catching and appealing to your readers. The design elements of typography, layout and design, graphics and art, and color will provide you with many ideas and techniques to incorporate into your reports. Desktop publishing techniques covered will give you the skills used by professionals in the printing industry.

keyboard entry of data, while the purpose of desktop publishing software was to merge both text and graphics and lay out the copy. Actually, the differences between word processing and desktop publishing software are fading. Word processing software can be used to design documents. Desktop publishing software can be used for ordinary, simple documents as well as highly sophisticated publications. Today, the two areas overlap extensively and are frequently used interchangeably.

This chapter provides a guide to determining the design of the document, or in plain words what your document is going to look like. The first part considers the main design elements of a document, and the last part examines various desktop publishing techniques.

In designing a document, four main elements should be considered: (1) typography, (2) layout and design, (3) graphics and art, and (4) color. Each of these areas will be discussed in detail.

> **Design Elements**
> - Typography
> - Layout and Design
> - Graphics and Art
> - Color

Typography

Typography is defined as the art and style of printing. The invention of the Selectric Typewriter in 1968 with an element rather than fixed type opened up a whole new array of publishing possibilities. By changing the element, type could be either elite (12 characters per inch) or pica (10 characters per inch) in size. The user also had the flexibility of several different type styles by changing elements–Prestige Elite, Courier, Letter Gothic, and a few others. But this process was somewhat limiting and also time-consuming.

Today users have at their disposal literally thousands (and more are being created) of typefaces and fonts from which to choose. The selection of type can set a psychological mood and style for a document. The size and weight of type can grab attention. A particular typeface can bring back memories from a familiar publication. Type can make a document more formal or informal or set a general tone. A few examples are shown of how typography choices can reflect a mood or create an atmosphere.

Before making your selection, a grasp of a few fundamental basics of typography is important. The vertical height of the lowercase x is referred to as x-height with the bottom of the main part of a letter called the baseline. The parts of a character that rise above the x-height are called ascenders, and the parts that fall below are descenders.

Additionally, you must determine the type format to be used on the computer. Type is available in two formats–PostScript and bit-mapped. Bit-mapped fonts are available in various sizes whereas PostScript fonts, like a good frying pan, fit all occasions. Whenever possible, PostScript fonts are a better choice because they are easily resized by the computer for whatever size is desired.

In working with type, you need to consider the kinds, size, spacing, alignment, and a variety of other type characteristics. The choices you make can greatly affect the impression your report makes–be sure that the impression is favorable and conveys the appropriate and desired message.

Kinds of Type

Type can be classified into many different categories. One category is *serif* or *sans serif*. Serif (a French word for tails) refers to the small cross strokes or flares at the ends of a letter's main stems. Even though sans serif (meaning without serifs) provides a cleaner, simpler look, some people believe that a serif type is more distinguished looking as well as easier to read.

Typeface refers to a specific type design. Typeface names may represent the name of the designer (Bodoni, Goudy, Zapf), where the designer lived (Chicago, London, New York), publications (London Times and Century Magazine), or a description of their character (Bookman and Avante Garde). Even professional typesetters usually limit their selections to two or three different typefaces.

A *type family* includes all the variations of a basic type design in every weight and point size. These variations, also called typestyle, include bold, italics or oblique, bold italics, shadow, outline, underline, and strikethru. Many typefaces are also available in condensed, narrow, or expanded versions. These variations are particularly helpful when the writer wants to say a lot in a small space or expand a few words to fill a larger space.

Another term used in specifying type is *font*. A font usually means a complete set of characters (the full alphabet, numbers, and symbols) in one weight and style of a typeface.

Sizes of Type

Type size is measured by using the language of printers–points and picas. A point (72 points equal an

Serif

Sans Serif

Plain
Bold
Italics
Bold Italics
Shadow
Outline
<u>Underline</u>
~~Strikethru~~
Compressed

. 5 7 9 **11 12**

14 18 24

36 48

72

This is an example of 10-point font using 15-point leading.

This is an example of 12-point font using 14-point leading.

0 tracking

20 tracking

-20 tracking

inch) is the smallest typographic unit of measurement. A pica is approximately 12 points or 1/6 of an inch.

On a computer, text can range from 2 points to extremely large sizes (see examples). However, the logical size for text body ranges from 8 points to 12 points. Headings are normally made in bold to capture the reader's attention and can vary in size to show the level of importance. In general, the larger the letters, the more important the heading.

Weight, meaning the thickness of the strokes making up the letters, is another choice affecting the size or look of a letter. Terms used to distinguish among weights in a typeface of a specific size are extra light, light, regular, medium, semibold, bold, extra bold, heavy, or ultrabold.

Type Spacing

Instead of the standard typewritten spacing of single, double, or triple spacing, line spacing can be varied for a more pleasing look. This particular copy is 12-point text size with 14 points of line spacing–frequently called *leading*, a leftover term from the days when type was formed from hot, liquid lead.

Computer type also has the capability of adding or subtracting horizontal spacing between words. The term *tracking* refers to overall spacing within a group of letters, a word, or a line or more of text. If spacing between letters appears to be uneven or if a tighter or looser fit is desired, tracking is available on many word processing or desktop publishing programs allowing you to add or delete space between letters.

Another way of adjusting space between letters is referred to as *kerning*–the adjustment of space between paired letters. Even though software provides automatic kerning, some paired letter combinations can sometimes be adjusted for a more pleasing appearance and better readability.

Kerning

VAL VAL
Yat Yat
Too Too

Type Alignment

Type alignment of left, right, centered, or justified is possible either before or after the words are keyed into the computer. Justification, making both the left and right margins flush, gives a report a blocked look and is preferred by some individuals. However, justification should not be used if it causes valleys or rivers of white space to run through the copy.

Hyphenating words, either through the software or by manually forcing words to be divided, can help to prevent spacing rivers and give the copy a tighter look. Hyphenation rules should be followed. Research has shown that readability is improved if a ragged right margin is used. The uneven line endings provide a visual crutch for the eyes in addition to giving a more artistic look to the page. The choice is one for personal judgement. (Take notice of how this book is done.)

Left

Centered

Right

Justified

However, justification should not be used if doing so causes   valleys or rivers of space to run through   the copy.

Other Type Terminology and Variations

Point size measures the distance from the lowest descender to the highest ascender, while the distance between one baseline and the next is called leading. A

ALL CAPS ARE HARD TO READ!

The use of the lowercase letters makes text much easier to read!

capital letter in 36-point type will not be 36 points high because capital letters have no ascenders or descenders.

Printed materials using lowercase are more distinctive because of ascenders–the part of the character rising above the body–and descenders–the tail, or part of the character sinking below the baseline. Therefore, putting words, phrases, lines, or paragraphs in all uppercase letters tends to make the words harder to read rather than easier to read.

> Because more than 95 percent of all written words are in lowercase letters, people can read faster when lowercase letters are used. Also, uppercase letters are less distinctive without the ascenders and descenders of lowercase letters.

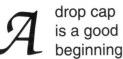

Reverse

Headings in reverse type–white or light characters on a dark background–offer an eye-catching combination for headings. However, too much reverse type can become difficult to read.

Another variation possible for the beginning of a chapter or a new section is the use of a drop cap–so-called because the baseline drops below the first line of text in the paragraph. In creating a drop cap, the software must have the capability of altering the line leading to accommodate the oversize letter and create an indent that is cancelled after a specified number of lines.

In addition to the alphabetic and numeric characters, the design of a typeface family must include many other characters–forms of punctuation; common diacritical marks; brackets, braces, and parentheses; em

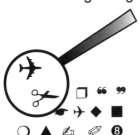

A drop cap is a good beginning

Examples of Zapf Dingbats

and en dashes; and a bar for building fractions. Manufacturers also create pi fonts with many special characters such as bullets, ballot boxes, check marks, and arrows. Specialty pi fonts are available for many fields including mathematics, science, music, television, and horse racing.

En dash –
Em dash —

Desktop Publishing Techniques—Typography

Desktop publishing techniques include and extend beyond the realm of typing rules. The typography techniques following are used by professional desktop publishers, typesetters, and printers to make documents look more professional.

- Use no more than two or three different fonts in any one document—possibly a sans serif for headings and a serif for the body (or a serif for the heading and a sans serif for the body).

- Experiment with different typestyles—bold, italics, shadow, outline, or a combination of these styles.

- Use italics rather than underlining the names of books or magazines.

- Remember to vary font size for better reading. For instance, if you have your name and address on three separate lines on the title page, use a larger size for whatever is the most important. Making all three lines the same size will not get the same attention.

- Remember to follow typing rules of word division when needed.

- Consider using one space between sentences as in professional typesetting rather than two as in typing.

- Use the en and em dashes. Instead of the two hyphens used on the typewriter for a dash, the em dash provides a more professional look. The method of accessing these keys may vary depending upon the type of software/hardware application used. Check your user's manual to find the special key-strokes for these keys.

  -     hyphen
  –   en dash
  —   em dash

- Use an ellipsis (...) to show omissions in a quote. Again, the method of accessing this keystroke may vary from program to program. Striking three periods also works.
  ...   ellipsis

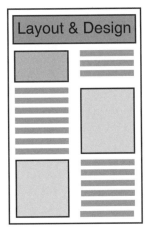

Layout and Design

In designing a document, layout and design of each and every page is required. Often it helps to envision what the final pages will look like by making a dummy or draft of the work. This procedure includes sketching in the basic parts.

Many considerations and decisions are required in creating a vision of the final document. These considerations are page size, placement, margins, column size, white space, headings and subheadings, and headers and footers.

Page Size

A first step is to determine the finished paper size. Most writers assume that they will print their document on standard 8 1/2 x 11 paper; however, many other possibilities are available. Even though laser printers accept only standard or legal-size paper, you are not necessarily held to these sizes because the output can be trimmed to a desired size by using a paper cutter.

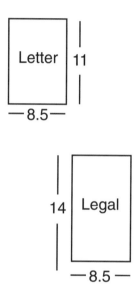

The printing industry has established recommended standards on sizes for books and periodicals. Because these standards are more familiar to readers and also make efficient use of paper trim sizes, you might want to consider and use these formats as guidelines for your document if you desire a size other than the standard or legal-paper size.

Book Page Sizes	
7 1/4" x 4 1/4"	Paperback Novel
8 1/2" x 5 1/2"	Half-Size Page Booklet
6" x 9"	Book Format
9 1/4" x 7 1/4"	Manual
8 1/2 x 11"	Standard Page
9" x 12"	Display Book

Periodical Sizes	
7" x 10"	Comic Book
8" x 11"	*Time* Magazine
8 1/2" x 11"	Newsletter, Magazine
9" x 12"	Magazine
10" x 14"	*Life* Magazine or Tabloids
11" x 17"	Tabloids/Small Newspapers

In addition to size, you need to decide on the orientation–portrait/vertical/tall or landscape/horizontal/wide–desired as your final output. People tend to use portrait because they are used to it; however, a landscape orientation might work very effectively.

Placement

Page design must be in balance. This balance can be created by using a symmetrical or asymmetrical design. In a symmetrical design arrangement, all elements are centered on the page. This style suggests formality, dignity, and reliability. In contrast, an asymmetrical design where image masses are placed informally may signify a more modern look.

Optical center is a consideration in the placement of material on a page. Optical center of a page is actually about a quarter of an inch above and a quarter of an inch to the left of the actual center of the paper.

A picture looks better if it is placed a bit higher than actual center within a picture frame. Similarly, a page is more attractive if the material is a bit higher than actual center.

Margins

Adequate margins should be left to give each and every page a frame or border. Top and bottom and left and right margins should all be even unless the document is to be bound. The amount of room left for the binding will vary according to the type of binding selected (see Chapter 7–"Finalizing Your Master-piece"). However, you must determine the type of binding desired before determining your margin settings. On a standard page of 8-1/2 x 11, you will normally need to allow a quarter of an inch to a half inch of extra space for the binding.

Column Size

Research has shown that it is possible to read faster and comprehend more information when shorter lines are used. The actual length of the line will, of course, depend upon the page size. If you are using standard size (8-1/2 x 11), you may want to consider using a columnar layout format. A columnar format is okay for a business report. You want the reader(s) to find it easy and pleasurable to read–not dull and boring.

A *basic single-column layout* is the common and traditional way. If you use one column, you will be better off to use 12-point type versus 10-point type. In using the smaller 10-point type, you need to leave additional leading between the lines to make the copy more readable.

A variation is to use one column but shorten the line length. A shorter line length not only makes the material easier and faster to read but also allows space for art, illustrations, quotes, annotations, captions, or even headings and subheadings. This book is an example of one column with space left on the *inside* (left on right-facing pages and right on left-facing pages). The headings and subheadings are left in the main or wide column, but the narrow column is open

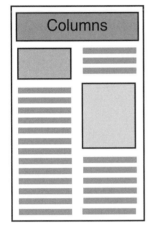

for a variety of different illustrations. This space can be left on either side; however, the author prefers to have the extra space left in the center near the binding; thus, the book can be read without losing the main content in the seams.

The use of *two- or three-column formats* gives a very professional look and increases the readability of the copy. A gutter space, which can vary in size, is left between the columns. Smaller types sizes of 9, 10, or 11 points is recommended whenever you are using a two- or three-column format. If copy is full justified, however, you need to check carefully to see if any words need to be divided to prevent valleys and rivers.

White Space

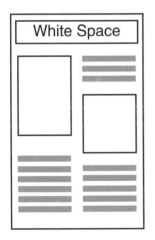

White space (or whatever color background is used) is very important for a professional look. Actually, each page should contain approximately 50 percent or more white space. Pages with too much type and art give the appearance of being too heavy and hard to read.

Headings and Subheadings

Headings and subheadings are crucial in helping the busy readers of today. Novels must flow along and keep readers enticed–or the reader will probably quit. However, nonfiction and business writing requires aids to help the readers keep focused. Remember that a reader may be interrupted with a phone call, visitor, or some other distraction–causing the mind to wander. Headings and subheadings can do wonders in helping to keep the reader focused as well as allow readers to scan the copy for parts that are of particular interest to them.

Headings and subheadings can be considered as the elements that make up an outline. Rules to follow in constructing these headings and subheadings are:

- Make heads and subheads concise but descriptive–possibly attention getting.

- Follow parallel construction–verb and noun or nouns only.

- Break the divisions down so that a heading or subheading always has two or more listings.

- Make the heads and subheads agree with the table of contents (if used), although a table of contents may omit minor subheads and list only two or three levels.

A hierarchy of sizes and styles is needed for showing the various levels of headings or subheadings. The plan should be consistent and logical and progress from higher to lower levels in an obvious pattern. For instance, a first-level subhead could use an 18-point, bold font. A second-level subhead could be reduced to 14-point bold. A third level could be 12-point bold italics. If a fourth-level subhead is needed, it could be an indented paragraph heading using italicized type the size of the regular body text. An illustration of this pattern follows:

First Level
Second Level
Third Level
Fourth Level

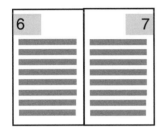

Page Numbers

Any time you have more than one or two pages, you need to number them. Computer software has the capability of performing this function automatically, but you must determine where you want the page numbers. Several choices are acceptable–either the upper or lower outside corners or the middle of the bottom of the page. Placing the numbers on the outside corners allows readers to locate a specific page more easily when scanning through a book.

If making facing copies–print on both sides of the page–you should follow a procedure used by professional printers. They always place odd numbers on the right-facing page and even numbers on the left-facing page. New sections or chapters should always start on a right-facing page. This procedure means that you may occasionally have a blank page before a new section or chapter.

Headers and Footers

In today's busy world, readers frequently scan written material rapidly rather than reading it thoroughly from front to back. These readers are helped in locating or identifying a particular section or area of a report if headers (identifying information at the top of a page) and footers (identifying information at the bottom of a page) are used. (Headers and footers should not be confused with footnotes, which are explained in Chapter 4.) Variations are possible, but one logical system is to have the left-facing page show the overall title and the right-facing page show the chapter or section title. Thus, a reader can quickly check the name of the document and also focus in on the specific subject.

Desktop Publishing Techniques–
Layout and Design

A few desktop publishing techniques for the layout and design of copy are as follows:

- Avoid long, boring paragraphs by using the technique of listing (enumerating) with a bullet, checkmark, arrow, or one of the other interesting characters available.

- Keep paragraphs fairly short (five or eight lines)–particularly when using two- or three-column layouts.

- Make your page breaks so that you avoid widow and orphan lines–one line stranded from the rest of the paragraph.

- Make documents with two or three columns all end evenly on the bottom of the page–vary the leading around sideheads, rewrite and add/delete a few words, or use other techniques to change the arrangement.

- Keep each page with approximately 50 percent white space. Pages with too much on them are not reader friendly.

Graphics and Art

Anything on a page other than text is usually referred to as graphics. Thus, graphics can include visual elements such as photographs, drawings, graphs, charts, icons, lines, boxes, patterns, and even background tints.

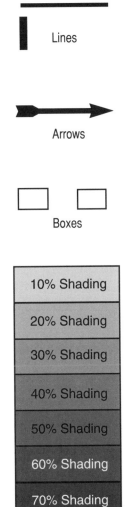

When used in a document, graphics and art should clarify, add to, illustrate, or enhance the document in some way. Graphics and art should not be used without a specific reason or purpose. Otherwise, the inclusion of graphics and art may be distracting and confusing rather than helpful to your readers. This discussion is going to classify visual elements into the two general areas of graphics and art.

Graphics

Graphics–including lines, boxes, patterns, and background tints–are helpful in making documents more stimulating and appealing to readers. Text line after text line can get boring. Lines, boxes, and shading are useful in creating divisions or focusing attention upon a given area. Icons or symbols available in various fonts may help focus or direct the reader's attention. Logos provide a subtle way of marketing your company or providing a theme for a product or topic.

Art

Art–including photographs, drawings, graphs, charts, or icons–enhances your document by creating interest or illustrating points made in the text. Art can be inserted in your document in two ways–by using either the traditional pasteup method or an electronic pasteup method.

In the traditional pasteup method, you simply leave space for the art. Before reproducing the copy on a duplicating machine, you paste the artwork in place.

In an electronic pasteup, you will have the entire document on disk and can make a copy or copies from the printer. Electronic art can come from a variety of sources and be imported into your document:

- Drawings or diagrams created on the computer from a draw or paint program such as Illustrator, FreeHand, Canvas, CorelDRAW, MacDraw, etc.

- Art created by someone else and sold as clip art that you can copy and paste into your document.

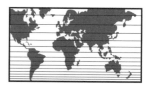

- Drawings or photos scanned into the computer using a special scanner–such work may need to be modified or retouched using a computer program such as Adobe PhotoShop.

- Graphs or charts created from a spreadsheet program such as Excel, Lotus 1-2-3, or Quattro Pro.

Desktop Publishing Techniques–Graphics and Art

Desktop publishing techniques helpful in the area of graphics and art are:

- Use art to enhance, illustrate, or provide additional information.

- Refer to a piece of art in the narration *before* it appears–not after.

- Size art to fit your needs but be sure that you keep proper proportions.

- Crop art to eliminate unwanted portions.

- Make sure that any art (including charts and graphs) is viewed at the same distance as the text–a reader should not have to hold a page closer or farther away to read a graph or other piece of art.

- Be sure that you have the legal rights for any art used. Clip art is legal as it is either public domain or commercial. Public domain art is not protected by copyright. When commercial collections are purchased, the user buys the clip art and a license for the right of unlimited use of the artwork.

- Create your own infographics–graphics such as those used in *USA Today*–to portray hard technical information in the form of a pie chart, bar chart, line chart, or scattergram.

- Remember that nondigitized art can be mechanically pasted up and reproduced on a copying machine or taken to a professional printer.

Color

Color adds a whole new look to a document. Henry Ford thought that the production of only black cars was sufficient. He was wrong. Today cars are manufactured in a wide variety of colors. Similarly, the public has not been satisfied with only black printing. Today, printers are available that will print in a full array of colors. The technology is advancing rapidly, and the price of having color printers connected to a computer is rapidly decreasing. You need to begin to think about using color. Even if your company does not have a color printer now, it probably will in the near future.

Overview

Color is a narrow band of the electromagnetic spectrum that falls between ultraviolet and infrared light. Although individuals perceive colors differently, the use of color creates moods, sensations, and impressions that can be effective in getting the desired results.

Colors are created by either adding or subtracting color depending whether they are obtained through a printing process or projected images–such as on a television or some type of projection screen. In printing, colors are obtained through a subtractive system. The three primary colors overlap in various ways resulting in secondary colors; black is the result when all three colors overlap. By contrast, colored lights of red, green, and blue projected in overlapping circles mix and form secondary colors, but when all three colors overlap, the result is white. The illustrations show the difference in these processes.

(Subtractive)
Printed Images

(Additive)
Projected Images

Printing

In the past, full-color printing was possible only through professional processors requiring four separate press runs because only one color of ink can be printed with each pass. Therefore, four plates are required, one for each of the four basic colors. The three colors of cyan (blue), magenta, and yellow, plus black, produce what appears to be all the colors of the visible spectrum. The process of making the negatives for the plates is called color separation, which can be done automatically with many desktop publishing computer application programs. Some of the software allows users to design a document in color on the screen. By simply checking color separations on the print dialog box, the computer will make a master for each of the primary colors. These masters are then taken to the printer where plates are made.

In today's technology, color computer printing is possible using ink jet, thermal, or laser printers. Copy machines capable of producing full-color copies are also available. Thus, full color for your document is a consideration. Originally, the Bible was painstakingly made by hand using color inks. Today document designers can return to this full-color practice at an affordable price using modern technology.

Paper

If color printers and copiers are not available to you at the present time, you still have the option of using colored paper. Light-tinted paper with black type is less glaring for readers. In addition, the use of a variety of colors of paper is helpful in coding your work. For instance, different sections can be produced in different colors or a variety of handouts can be made in a variety of colors for easier distinguishing and referencing.

In a recent innovation, several companies are now selling paper with a variety of color designs already printed on the paper. With several of the companies, you can purchase a computer template enabling you to see the color design on the screen. Print, graphics, and art can then be planned and keyed aesthetically around the color designs. When you insert the color-designed paper into the tray of the computer, you are able to run black print onto the design. The result is the look of a full-color document; yet, you are using only your regular black-and-white printer.

Colored Paper

- Prevents Glare
- Codes Pages
- Adds Variety

The original company marketing such products is PaperDirect. Contact them at 1-800-A-PAPERS for a catalog showing a variety of designed papers to be used in printing.

Output Results

If you have a full-color printer available, you can create very attractive and effective documents. However, producing documents in color may seem similar to learning to color again–similar to what you went through as a child.

Decisions must be made. In general, for most documents you will want to use a light background with dark type and objects. Full-color clip art is available for importing into your documents. If you do not now have color printer and copy capabilities available, you may in a few years. The competitive edge of the business world relies on technology. Presently, a revolution is underway in using color for presentations, and the use of color for documents will become more and more available in the near future.

Desktop Publishing Techniques–Color

In using color in your reports, the following desktop publishing techniques regarding color may be of help to you:

- Be sure that you have the capability of reproducing in color at an affordable price before planning and making your report in color.

- Limit the use of color to about three or four pages unless full color is used.

- Use a sufficient contrast for effective reading–dark print on light background or light print on dark background.

- Make objects in their proper color–such as a red Santa Claus and a red, white, and blue American flag.

- Remember that approximately 10 percent of all males and a lesser number of females are color deficient or color blind–red and green used side by side may look like one gray blob.

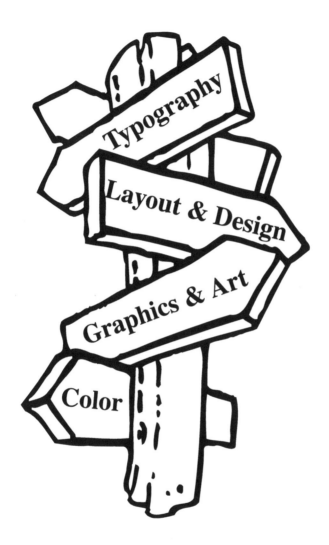

The Signposts of Document Design

The Bottom Line

Desktop publishing your report can make a typically boring report into an attractive, professional-looking report. This strategy may give you the competitive edge in getting attention and selling your ideas.

Your report still requires the traditional tasks of preparation, including planning, organizing, and researching along with the development of writing style and mechanics. Resources must be credited properly. A last step is completing your masterpiece with a final proofreading and editing effort and enhancing the report by making appropriate printing and binding decisions.

The next chapter will help you finalize your masterpiece. The polish you apply in selecting the paper and binding and in proofreading and editing can make a difference.

Read this Diagnostic Glimpse before Chapter 7.

Diagnostic Glimpse #7

How can you finalize your masterpiece?

How carefully do you need to read Chapter 7, "Finalizing Your Masterpiece"? The questions below will help you discover how much you already know about enhancements as well as accuracy and meticulousness.

Agree	Disagree	1.	Paper and binding issues should be determined after writing a report.	
Agree	Disagree	2.	All reports should be produced on white paper.	
Agree	Disagree	3.	Research has found that colored plastic overlays used on books produce better reading results for all readers.	
Agree	Disagree	4.	Papers with a high rag or cotton content age better with less deterioration in color and context.	
Agree	Disagree	5.	A matte or dull finish grade of paper provides a more sophisticated look and is better for halftones and color printing.	
Agree	Disagree	6.	A ream of 20 lb. paper weighs 20 pounds.	
Agree	Disagree	7.	Paper is either grain short or long and also has a right and wrong side.	
Agree	Disagree	8.	Reports should always be printed on a laser printer.	
Agree	Disagree	9.	Facing pages should be numbered on the inside.	
Agree	Disagree	10.	Editing and proofreading are essentially the same process.	

1. disagree
2. disagree
3. agree
4. agree
5. disagree
6. disagree
7. agree
8. disagree
9. disagree
10. disagree

see pages 121 and 122

Name types of errors to look for during proofreading.

use a ruler
read out loud
read a line backwards
limit time
read when fresh
avoid interruptions

List six techniques to use when proofreading.

substance
style
consistency

List three things to consider during editing.

stapled cover sheet
stapled report cover
two-pocket portfolio
prong-style report cover
punchless cover
vinyl ring binder
VeloBind
thermal binding
plastic spiral binding
wire ring

Give various methods of binding a report.

matte
coated

Name two types of paper finish.

color
paper
printing
cover
binding

List five ways of enhancing your report.

Diagnostic Glimpse #7

Finalizing Your Masterpiece

While the contents of a report are important, other factors can make or break your report. Do not believe the statement, "You can't judge a book by its cover." A book is judged by its cover as well as many other seemingly small details.

You are not through with your report yet. The way it looks is very important. Before you stamp *completed* on your report, consider a few more details.

Prior to printing the report, you need to select a type of paper and binding. In addition, proofreading and editing are necessary before your report is a polished product.

Enhancements

Many of the modern desktop publishing techniques and design features suggested in Chapter 6 can help in designing your report. Also, Chapter 5 covers the various formats or looks that a report can have.

Additional enhancements of size, paper, color, printing, cover, and binding can give a report enough added polish to make it both attractive and attention getting.

Color

Reports do not have to be an all white (visually stark) affair. Although most reports and books are printed with black ink on white paper, many other choices are available.

If photos are included in the report, a very white paper will show the light highlights better and make the dark inks seem darker. On the other hand, you may want to use paper that is slightly off-white—natural, cream, ivory, eggshell, mellow, or soft white—to reduce the glare in very technical manuals that require readers to spend a considerable amount of reading time.

A researcher found, in a study of visual factors contributing to reading disability, that colored plastic overlays—particularly blue and gray—used on books can produce immediate and dramatic effects on the reading performance of children who are reading disabled or dyslexic. In fact, all readers did better with the plastic overlays (Miller, 1990).

Color is useful in coding material. For instance, color coding is useful for the following situations:

- Make different sections different colors for quick identification.

- Use a different color for a glossary or the appendix to allow for easy referencing.

- Use a different color page for the section or chapter heading of each new section.

- Use color for the cover and a neutral white, off-white, or beige for the inside.

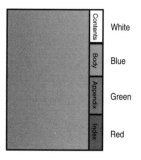

The use of color tabs to identify sections.

Paper

Paper comes in different types and sizes. The quality of the paper reflects the professionalism of the report.

Type. Papers with a high rag or cotton content are more expensive but age better with less deterioration in color and context. Thus, a report to be kept on file for many years should be printed with 100 percent rag or cotton content. Papers made without any rag content are more economical and good only for reports that will be read and sent to the recycling bin within a short time.

Categories. Numerous categories are used in classifying paper. For reports, the main categories to consider are book or text papers, cover papers, and bond. Book and text papers are used in printing and are made mainly from sulfate pulp. Bond is considered more of an office paper but may range from 100 percent rag to low-grade paper using ground wood. Cover papers are heavier weight papers used for the covers of pamphlets, journals, and paperback books.

Grades. Paper for printing comes either uncoated or coated. Uncoated paper, also referred to as offset paper, is available in a wide variety of colors, weights, and quality levels. Such paper comes in either rough or smooth surface. Antique and vellum are relatively rough, while lustre and English are fairly smooth. Offset or uncoated paper provides good printing results at minimum cost for copy with line art–no halftones.

Coated paper has a slicker, higher-end impression than uncoated or offset paper and is used for catalogs, magazines, and upscale brochures or reports. The final finish of coated papers may be matte–a dull finish–or glossy, a shiny finish.

A glossy paper provides a more sophisticated look and is better for halftones and color printing. Even without halftones, however, printing on coated paper will be clearer. For instance, the narrow rules and fine serifs will show a crisper look than if you printed on offset paper.

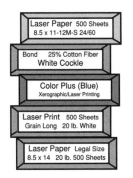

Weight. The weight of paper is referred to as *basis* for book and cover papers and *substance* for bond papers. The basis or substance weight of paper is determined by weighing 500 sheets of a paper in its basic size, which is 25 by 38 inches for text paper, 20 by 26 inches for cover paper, and 17 by 22 for bond paper. (When bond paper is cut, the result is four stacks of 8 1/2-by-11 sheets. Thus, the weight of four reams of paper represents the substance weight.)

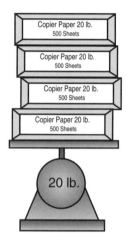

4 Reams = X lb.

As a result of these varied sizes, you may run into difficulties in referring to paper by its weight. For instance, a 50-pound book paper is equal in weight to 27-pound cover or 20-pound bond papers.

Heavier weight paper is more costly but not necessarily thicker. Rough sheets of paper are thicker than smooth ones, and a matte finish is thicker than a gloss finish.

Opacity. Before printing on both sides of paper, you need to check the opacity of the paper being used. Opacity refers to the degree to which printing or writing on one side of a sheet will show through to the other side.

Other Factors. A few other factors are important in choosing and using your paper. Consider using recycled paper. Paper companies now offer colorful recycled paper at a cost savings to you and your company. In addition to producing your report on attractive less-expensive paper, you will doing your part in saving the forests.

A ream of paper is usually marked either grain long or grain short on the package with words or an arrow. Paper tends to tear and fold more easily with the grain of the paper. The grain direction should be parallel with the binding edge; otherwise, the pages turn less easily and do not lie flat.

Also, the right and the wrong side of the paper is referred to as the felt (usually the smoother side) or the wire side. Therefore, if only one side of the paper is to be used, printing should be on the right side. When you place the ream so that you can read the label, the right side of the paper will be on top.

Printing

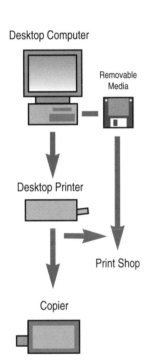

Desktop Computer

Removable Media

Desktop Printer

Print Shop

Copier

Printing is frequently accomplished by sending the document from the computer to a desktop printer. Depending upon the individual circumstances, you may find it more desirable to print a small number of copies on your desktop printer rather than going to a copier. However, in many situations, you may prefer to print one copy on your desktop printer and the rest on your office copier. The choice frequently depends upon the number of copies needed and the availability of each type of equipment.

Larger quantities should be printed on a high-volume copier or an offset printing press to keep printing costs down. For better quality, a print shop may prefer to receive removable media (disks or cartridges) rather than a paper master.

Laser printers may be either 300 or 600 dpi (dots per inch). The output from a 600 dpi printer has a more professional and finished look–especially if your report contains graphics.

Cover

A customized cover on a report can set it apart. Other reasons for using a cover on a report are because it is to be read by many people or saved for a long period of time. Studies by General Binding Corporation show that a report is twice as likely to be read and three times as likely to be saved if it is attractively bound.

The cover of a report can vary from ordinary title pages, to front and back pages using cover paper, to specially ordered personalized notebooks. The budget, the available timeline, the importance of the report, and how the report will be used are all factors to consider.

Binding

In deciding on a cover, you also need to consider the method of binding your report. Important questions to consider are:

- Is a good image important?

- How many pages are in each report?

- How many reports are to be produced?

- Are revisions going to be necessary?

- How many people will be handling the report?

- Will the report be inserted into a file?

- Does the report include items the reader may fill out and remove?

- What binding possibilities are available?

- What does the budget allow?

After answering these questions, you are ready to look into various methods of binding reports. These methods, along with a few comments on each, are:

- Stapled cover sheet–least expensive for a report with 20 pages or less.

- Stapled report covers–file folder with two perforated notches in the center seam; inexpensive and easily filed.

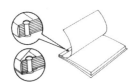

Prong

Ring

- Two-pocket portfolios–available in a variety of different kinds of finishes and colors; can personalize a large number by having company logo, name, address, phone number printed on them; can use pocket on one side for report and the other for pictures, brochures, business cards, and other accompanying materials.

- Prong-style report covers and fasteners–similar to the two-pocket portfolios but uses prongs to fasten report into the center.

- Punchless covers–no holes need be punched; good for reports where changes may need to be made; good only for a limited number of pages.

- Vinyl ring binders–standardized three-ring binders available in a variety of sizes, colors, and textures; good for use where the adding or deletion of pages is needed; can be personalized with printing if a large amount will be needed; binders are available with a clear plastic sheet to insert your own cover sheet easily, inexpensively, and tailored to a particular report.

- VeloBind systems–requires the purchase of a machine; very professional looking reports; easily filed; cannot update pages. In VeloBinding, the pages are machine punched with tiny holes. Plastic spines are then put in place and machine pressed with plastic rivets.

- Thermal binding systems–requires the purchase of a machine; good for reports of different sizes; cannot update pages; very professional appearance. The covers are purchased with beads of glue already on the inside of the spine. The document is placed inside the folder. The folder is then placed inside the machines which melts the glue to the edges of the paper.

- Plastic spiral binding–requires purchase of a machine; reports will lie perfectly flat when open, very professional appearance; can update report with machine by adding or deleting pages.

- Wire ring–requires purchase of a machine; front cover can be folded underneath the back cover for easy reading; possible (but hard) to update report.

Plastic Spiral

Wire Ring

Binding is that added step that can make a good first impression. Because different amounts of margins need to be left for the different types of binding, the binding method *should be chosen before printing the final copies.* Many of the methods require additional space on the left-hand side. Equally important is the decision of whether to print front to back. When printing on the back side of the page in a bound report, the page number needs to be placed on the outside edge and the extra space for the margin will be needed on the right side of the page instead of the left. In desktop publishing programs, left and right pages are known as facing pages. The page you are now reading is a left facing page.

A wider margin allows space for binding.

Facing Pages

Accuracy and Meticulousness

The appearance of your report does make a difference; however, you must have the right content in the report for it to be effective. A most important aspect of a report is the quality of the writing. Little errors can make a big difference–the unfavorable kind. Therefore, the final step in completing a report is to edit and proofread your report carefully.

If possible, ask other people to look over the report for you. You might want to assign them

A good report relies on both content and context.

different tasks–similar to those performed by the staff in publishing a book. Terms used in the publishing world are *copyedit, copyread, edit, proofread,* etc. For reports, the terms *edit* and *proofread* are going to be used to discuss the steps needed to make sure that your report is accurate as well as meticulous in its final form.

Edit

Three different types of editing are required for any report. Even though these can be done by you or another person, it may be better to think of these as three separate tasks. Trying to do everything at once is hard; most people have trouble completing three things at the same time.

Substance. Before giving the report a more detailed scrutiny, a general content look is needed. Questions under consideration during this editing process are as follows:

- Is the material complete?
- Should any of the content be omitted?
- Is the information correct?
- Is the content presented in the right order?
- Is any reorganization needed?
- Are there better ways of presenting some of the information, such as graphs, tables, artwork, etc.?
- Does any rewriting need to be done?

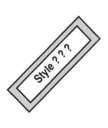

Style. Several types of style should be considered during the editing. First, is the writing consistent with the recommended styles of writing described in Chapter 2 and the style manuals for referencing discussed in Chapter 4? Next, have the styles or rules of your particular company been followed properly? Some companies have their own corporate style guides. If so, you will want to be in line with their desires.

Consistency. Another type of editing involves looking for consistency. Details in style should be consistent; possibly several ways are correct but one way should be chosen and used throughout the report. Other types of consistency are listed under the next section on proofreading.

Proofread

Proofreading your own work is hard and not very efficient. Because you are so familiar with the report, you tend to race through and think of the bigger picture, the next report, the visuals you need to make when you present the report, or whatever. Someone else who has not been working on the report can give it a much fresher and more efficient look.

If you do not have others available and are forced to be the one and only proofreader of your own work, you may want to use some special proofing techniques. These techniques would also be good for your proofreaders to follow.

- Use a ruler to slow down your reading and make yourself read line by line.

- Read the report out loud. This process slows down your reading and makes you listen to how it really sounds.

- Read each line backwards. The work will not make sense, but typographical errors will stand out more.

- Limit your proofreading to small bits at any one time. For instance, you can set a limit of only two pages in any one sitting. If time permits, you could limit yourself to a section or chapter a day.

- Proofread when you are most fresh. This time may be early morning or whatever time of the day is your peak for best performance.

- Try to proofread when you know you will have peace and quiet and can avoid interruptions from the telephone or visitors.

During proofreading, you and your other proofreaders may find the following list helpful in looking for errors.

- Does the report make sense?

- Are there any typographical errors?

- Are words divided correctly throughout the document?

- If right justification is used, should any words be force-hyphenated to prevent rivers and valleys of space in the lines?

- Are words on the first and last lines of a page or paragraph divided?

- Are there any orphan or widow lines?

- Is the style consistent throughout—fonts, spacing, indenting, headings, etc.?

- Is capitalization correct and consistent?

- Is spelling correct and consistent?

- Are numbers either given as figures or written out correctly and consistently?

- Do quotation marks and parentheses always have both a beginning and an ending?
- Do verbs and subjects agree?
- Is the correct word used in words that sound alike–their and there; two, to, and too; sense and cents, its and it's, etc.?
- Are complete sentences used and do they make sense?
- Are all numbers accurate?
- Are all totals correctly added?

7 Elements of a High-Impact Report

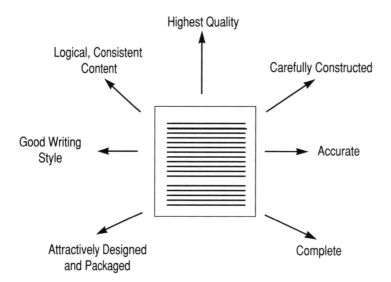

The Bottom Line

What you say is important! But how you say it and how it looks are also vital in creating a high-impact business report.

Your report can be enhanced by its color, paper, print, cover, and binding. Some of these decisions–such as the binding method–should be considered early in your report preparation to keep from limiting your selections or making extra work for yourself. However, many enhancements are the last step.

The accuracy and meticulousness of a report reflect on you and on your attention to detail. Would you hire a carpenter with a sloppy written proposal? Would you hire a secretary who used poor grammar in the letter of application? Would you grant monies to a proposal writer with inaccurate figures?

Yes, the image does make a difference. With the use of various enhancements and by being accurate and meticulous, you can finalize your masterpiece to properly showcase your report and get the results you want–provided the content is also there.

Reference

Miller, Sue. (December 14, 1990). "One Simple Device Helps Dyslexics to Read Better." *Los Angeles Times,* E24.

Glossary

Creating high-impact reports today requires a merging of terminology from the areas of communication, computers, and graphic design. This appendix provides a glossary of words used in the book.

A

Abstract　A page or less summary of the entire report. Also referred to as executive summary.

Active writing　A direct and dynamic method of writing with the subject doing the acting.

Appendix　Supporting material placed in the back of the report.

Art　Images of some type–may be *clip art*, original art, or photos.

Ascender　The part of a type character (b, d, f, h, k, l, and t) that extends above the height of a lower-case x.

B

Baseline　The imaginary line on which the bottom of the letters rest.

Bias-free language　Language avoiding the discrimination of gender, race, religion, age, disability, or ethnic group.

Bibliography   A list of writings on a subject.

Binding   The method of assembling a report for presentation–such as stapling or placing in ring or plastic binders.

Bit-mapped   Images (pictures or fonts) made up of individual dots, as opposed to lines or other shapes.

Body   The main part of the report.

Budget   The amount of financial help available for completing a report–includes time, help, equipment, and supplies.

Bullet   A dot, arrow, box, or some type of symbol used in a listing.

C

Classification of reports   The reason for the report–such to as inform, interpret, recommend, or persuade.

Clip art   Illustrations available commercially in digital form.

Coherence   Writing that flows along without abrupt changes.

Color   The reflection or absorption of light by a particular surface. Additive color is used in projected images, while subtractive color is used in printed images.

Column   Formats using one, two, or three vertical groupings on a page–similar to newspaper formats.

Conciseness   Writing without irrelevant information, redundancies, clutter, implied ideas, or abstract words.

Contents   A list in the beginning of a report showing the various headings and subheadings along with page references. Also referred to as *table of contents*.

Cover letter/memo   A letter (if external) or a memo (if internal) going along with a report briefly explaining the purpose of the report. (See definition for *transmittal letter*.)

D

Data collection   The task of finding or locating information needed for a report.

Descender   The part of a type character (g, j, p, q, and y) extending below the baseline of a lowercase x.

Desktop publishing   The process of producing publication-quality materials, such as reports, brochures, newsletters, etc., with a desktop computer system (computer, *laser printer*, page layout software, and *clip art*).

Digital   A format used by a computer system that scans the image into computer bits.

Dingbat A decorative character or symbol (such as a star, flower, pointing hand) used for bulleted lists, borders, or decoration.

Direct quotation   The exact words of another person.

E

Edit   Going over a report correcting for substance, style, and consistency.

Ellipsis   Three dots used to show the omission of parts of a quotation (. . .).

Em   A unit of measure in printing meaning the square of the body size of any type.

Emphasis   Giving either a word or a whole sentence more attention.

En   A printing term meaning half the space of an *em*.

Endnotes   A complete listing of the sources in numerical order at the end of a report. Endnotes are indicated in the text by a raised number or with a number in parenthesis. Eliminates the need for footnotes at the bottom of the page.

Enhancements   Additional ways—such as paper, printing, binding, etc.—of making a report a masterpiece.

Executive summary   A page or less abstract of the entire report. See *abstract*.

Expletive   Meaningless words such as "it is," "there are," "it is noted that," etc.

F

Facing pages   Pages with printing on both the front and back sides, such as in a book.

Font   A set of characters (the full alphabet, numbers, and symbols) in one weight and style of a typeface.

Footers   Identifying information at the bottom of each page.

Footnote   A reference at the bottom of the page for information in the report shown with a raised number in the text.

Format   A selection for the look of a report such as letter or memo, form, manuscript, *newsletter*, brochure, magazine, booklet, or manual.

GH

Glossary   A list of specialized words or terms with their meanings.

Graphics   Image enhancements, such as lines, boxes, backgrounds, art, *clip art*, scanned images, etc., used to create interesting and appealing visual design.

Headers   Identifying information placed at the top of each page of the report.

Heading   Main topics of the report.

IJK

Index   A list in the back of a long report or book to help readers find the page of a specific topic.

Kerning   The adjustment of space between paired letters such as an A and a V (AV).

L

Landscape   A page orientation where printing is aligned horizontally on the long edge of the paper (for standard-size paper, the 11-inch side is at the top). See *portrait*.

Laser printer   A computer printer that converts information from the computer into images using a laser to write on a photosensitive drum. The sensitized drum picks up toner and transfers it to a sheet of paper of film, much like a plain paper copier.

Leading   The vertical spacing between lines of text, measured in points. Also referred to as "line spacing."

MN

Masterpiece   A report that is outstanding.

Masthead   Identifying information on the first page of a *newsletter*.

Newsletter   A short newspaper-like publication–usually referring to pages using two- or three-columnar formats.

O

Objective(s)   The purpose(s) or reason(s) for the report.

Optical center   A location on the page slightly above and to the left of actual center.

Outline   *(noun)* A list of topics arranged in the most logical sequence. *(verb)* The task of completing a logical sequence of topics.

PQ

Paraphrasing   Quoting a source in your own words.

Parenthetical reference   A shortened reference placed in parentheses within the text, followed by a complete listing at the end of the section, chapter, or report.

Passive writing   Writing where the subject is a thing rather than a person.

Pi characters   Special characters that are not part of the normal font.

Plan   A method of attacking work such as the writing of a report.

Point   The smallest typographic unit of measurement for typefaces and lines. One inch contains 72 points.

Portrait   A page orientation where printing is aligned vertically on the short edge of the paper (for standard-size paper, the 8 1/2-inch side is at the top). See *landscape.*

PostScript   Images or fonts that use a page description language using outlines rather than a dot matrix method of forming characters, giving you the ability to scale or use other special effects.

Primary sources   Original materials, such as surveys, interviews, letters, diaries, etc.

Printing   The method of making hard copies such as *laser printer*, copier, or offset press.

Problem statement   A statement explaining "what" the report is intended to provide or solve such as more information, interpretation, recommendations, or a persuasive pitch.

Proofread   The task of looking for various types of errors in the report.

Purpose   The "why" of a report.

R

Readability   The ease of reading a report.

References   A list showing where information was obtained.

Researching   The act of obtaining information, such as going to the library, interviewing people, conducting a survey, etc.

Resources   A list showing where additional information can be found.

Reverse type   White or light characters on a dark background.

S

Sans serif   *Typeface* characters designed without *serifs* (small strokes on the ends of the main character stems).

Secondary sources   Information found in books, periodicals, and other publications.

Serif   Fine cross strokes or flares at the ends of the main stems on a letter.

Shading   The amount of screening used on *fonts*, art, or background, such as 70 percent.

Subheading   A topic placed under a major heading.

T

Table of contents   A list in the beginning of a report showing the various headings and subheadings along with page references. Also referred to as *contents*.

Target audience   The type of readers who will be reading the report.

Thumbnails   Small miniatures of a page.

Time schedule   A plan for completing a task such as a report.

Title page   A page with identifying information, such as the title, author, company, date, etc., of a report.

Tone   The mood of a report.

Tracking   The overall spacing within text. Tracking can be adjusted, especially for headlines and titles, when spacing between letters appears uneven.

Traditional manuscript   A manuscript produced on a typewriter.

Transmittal letter   A letter going along with a report briefly explaining the report along with why the report is being sent.

Type   See *typeface*.

Type alignment   Arrangement or positioning of type elements with respect to left and right margins (flush left, centered, flush right, or justified).

Type family   All the variations of a basic type design in every weight and point size.

Type style   Individual variations of a typeface, such as plain, bold, italic, underscore, shadow, and outline.

Typeface   A specific type design, such as Times Roman or Garamond. Some people use the terms *typeface* and *font* interchangeably.

Typography   The art of producing words and symbols from type. Also, the terminology and rules for using different typefaces.

UVWXYZ

Variety   Variation in order to prevent monotony.

White space   Empty space on a page. Each page should contain approximately 50 percent or more white space.

Word spacing   Horizontal spacing between words created by the spacebar on the keyboard. While this spacing is automatically set in relation to the typeface and size selected, it can be adjusted with some software.

Writing mechanics The proper use of abbreviations and acronyms, capitalization, italics, numbers, punctuation, spelling, and word division.

Writing style The way ideas are expressed on the written page.

Sample Reports

With the technological advances available today, reports can be produced on a desktop computer that do not look like the traditional reports of yesterday. This section provides reduced-size samples of a report in four different formats.

Example 1–Modern
A modern report takes advantage of the ability to add lines and boxes, change font size, and use italics. Otherwise, the format is basically the same as the traditional reports produced on typewriters.

Example 2–Ultra-Modern
The ultra-modern report adds one additional feature–a two-column format. Research shows that reading is enhanced by columns that are about an alphabet and a half long.

Example 3–Enhanced Modern
In the enhanced modern report, images can be manipulated and added. The purpose of the images should be to illustrate, provide supporting information, or create and gain interest.

Example 4–Traditional
The traditional report is the kind produced on typewriters–*in days of old*. Are you still awake?

Today's technology–including desktop computers, laser printers, desktop publishing software, clip art, etc.– provides capabilities previously not possible. The formats of all four report samples illustrated in Appendix B are possibly acceptable. But, why produce a traditional report when your report can look like the other three samples? Many combinations and exciting options are available.

Example 1–Modern

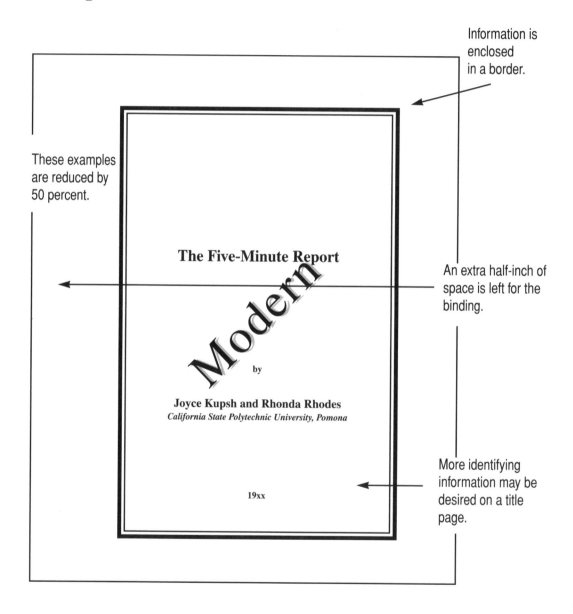

Information is
enclosed
in a border.

These examples
are reduced by
50 percent.

The Five-Minute Report

Modern

by

Joyce Kupsh and Rhonda Rhodes
California State Polytechnic University, Pomona

19xx

An extra half-inch of
space is left for the
binding.

More identifying
information may be
desired on a title
page.

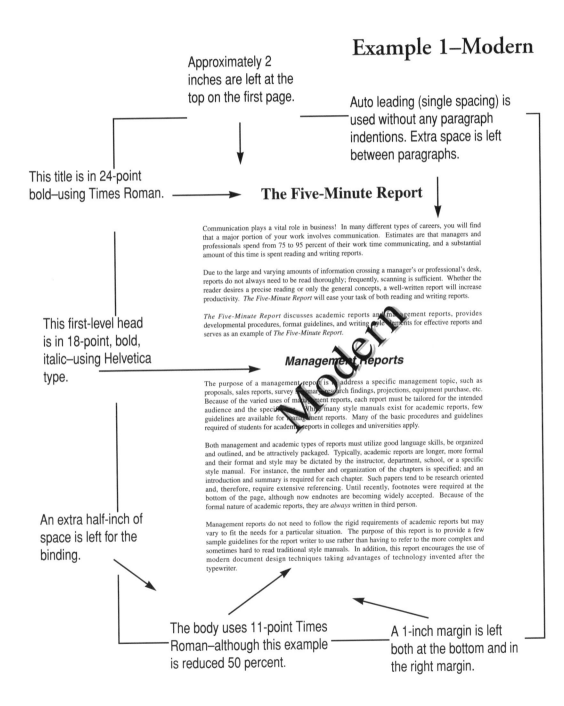

Example 1–Modern

Approximately 2 inches are left at the top on the first page.

Auto leading (single spacing) is used without any paragraph indentions. Extra space is left between paragraphs.

This title is in 24-point bold–using Times Roman.

The Five-Minute Report

This first-level head is in 18-point, bold, italic–using Helvetica type.

Communication plays a vital role in business! In many different types of careers, you will find that a major portion of your work involves communication. Estimates are that managers and professionals spend from 75 to 95 percent of their work time communicating, and a substantial amount of this time is spent reading and writing reports.

Due to the large and varying amounts of information crossing a manager's or professional's desk, reports do not always need to be read thoroughly; frequently, scanning is sufficient. Whether the reader desires a precise reading or only the general concepts, a well-written report will increase productivity. *The Five-Minute Report* will ease your task of both reading and writing reports.

The Five-Minute Report discusses academic reports and management reports, provides developmental procedures, format guidelines, and writing style elements for effective reports and serves as an example of *The Five-Minute Report*.

Management Reports

The purpose of a management report is to address a specific management topic, such as proposals, sales reports, survey summary, research findings, projections, equipment purchase, etc. Because of the varied uses of management reports, each report must be tailored for the intended audience and the specific goal. While many style manuals exist for academic reports, few guidelines are available for management reports. Many of the basic procedures and guidelines required of students for academic reports in colleges and universities apply.

Both management and academic types of reports must utilize good language skills, be organized and outlined, and be attractively packaged. Typically, academic reports are longer, more formal and their format and style may be dictated by the instructor, department, school, or a specific style manual. For instance, the number and organization of the chapters is specified; and an introduction and summary is required for each chapter. Such papers tend to be research oriented and, therefore, require extensive referencing. Until recently, footnotes were required at the bottom of the page, although now endnotes are becoming widely accepted. Because of the formal nature of academic reports, they are *always* written in third person.

Management reports do not need to follow the rigid requirements of academic reports but may vary to fit the needs for a particular situation. The purpose of this report is to provide a few sample guidelines for the report writer to use rather than having to refer to the more complex and sometimes hard to read traditional style manuals. In addition, this report encourages the use of modern document design techniques taking advantages of technology invented after the typewriter.

An extra half-inch of space is left for the binding.

The body uses 11-point Times Roman–although this example is reduced 50 percent.

A 1-inch margin is left both at the bottom and in the right margin.

Example 1–Modern

A header shows the title of the report and the page number. A line separates the header from the report

---

The Five-Minute Report   2

Developmental Procedures

Effective reports do not just happen; they must be very carefully developed. In developing or producing a report, the following topics need to be considered and addressed.

Outline

An outline is the first and most important step in developing a report. A well-prepared outline is the basis for all effective reports. If proper time and effort are devoted to ensuring that the outline is complete and parallel, writing the report becomes a matter of expanding the outline.

Table of Contents

The table of contents (or simply contents) is actually a listing of the outline with page numbers. If the report is over five pages, a table of contents with page numbers is strongly suggested. In addition, when numerous subheadings are used in a short report, a listing of the contents can help the reader locate specific information quickly.

Second-level headings are 14-point bold with more spacing before than after.

Title Page

Identification of a report should include the title of the report, the author's name and position, the class (or department or organization), the date, and any other pertinent information. A title page is probably the best place to place this information.

Transmittal Letter or Memo

A standard practice is to write a letter (if the intended audience is outside the organization) or a memo (if the intended audience is inside the organization) to accompany the report. This communication is directed to a specific person, personalized by using the YOU approach, and written in first person. The transmittal letter or memo may explain the purpose, content, and conclusions of the report. Or, the transmittal communication may be simply a cover note explaining things such as why the report is being sent, what is expected of the recipient, etc.

Executive Summary or Abstract

An executive summary or an abstract of a report serves the purpose of providing the readers a synopsis or overview of the report. An effective executive summary or abstract provides readers a clear, concise statement of what the report contains. According to Himstreet, Baty, and Lehman (1993), an executive summary is helpful regardless of the length and complexity of the report, because of the increased volume of information that managers must review.

Example 1–Modern

Since an executive summary or an abstract should be written to stand alone, it can be used as by itself in another publication as well as a part of the report. The general goal is to present the main point or to give the gist of the contents (Pauley and Riordan, 1990).

Word Processing or Desktop Publishing

The use of word processing software is the modern and productive way to generate reports. Because of features such as easy corrections, cut and paste, reformatting, spelling checks, etc., a higher quality report with less effort is possible (Lundgren, 1988).

The term desktop publishing was coined when small (desktop) computers became capable of accomplishing tasks previously performed only by professional typesetters. Actually desktop publishing can be performed using word processing software. However, desktop publishing software contains specialized features allowing users to perform tasks easier and better. As word processing packages keep becoming more sophisticated, the line of distinction between word processing and desktop publishing becomes blurred. Perhaps a better term to use is the more generic one of document design.

Packaging

Good content is of utmost importance. However, if the packaging is not attractive and efficient, the report may not make a positive impact. In general, packaging consists of the type of paper, document design, and the binding. A good analogy is of a person appearing for a job interview in a business office with uncombed hair and in casual wear attire.. The job applicant has made a negative impression before a single word is spoken.

Format Guidelines

A few common format guidelines are mentioned next. Additional questions or problems can be solved by referring to an accepted style manual.

Headings

A specific plan should be determined and adopted for a report. This report example uses a plan in which all topics listed first in the outline and contents are centered headings. For a second level, a side heading is used. If a third level is needed, paragraph headings can be used. Paragraph headings can be flush with the left margin or indented as shown in the next paragraph.

A third-level heading is in 12-point bold, italics and indented with the paragraph.

Purpose. Side headings and paragraph headings alert the reader to the upcoming topic, focus attention on the topic, and provide a vehicle to readers wishing to scan the report. If more than a half page appears without a sideheading, perhaps the outline and contents should be expanded. Reading paragraph after paragraph without sideheadings and subtitles is more difficult to red and becomes monotonous. Headings and sideheadings not only break the monotony of continuous paragraphs but keep the reader on track.

Example 1–Modern

The Five-Minute Report   **4**

═══

  Format Rules. The main rule of formatting is consistency within the report. The body of this report in the *Modern Style* follows the specifications as shown below:

Body Text	11-point Times
Main Title	24-point Times, Bold
1st-Level Head	18-point Helvetica, Bold, Italic, Centered
2nd-Level Head	14-point Helvetica, Bold, Left
3rd-Level Head	12-point Helvetica, Bold, Italic, Indented

Material is listed in a tabular format.

Paragraph Length

Beware! Paragraphs should contain only one idea or topic. If a paragraph is twelve lines or more, perhaps it contains more than one idea and should be divided. However, a paragraph is not complete unless it consists of a least two sentences.

Spacing

Contrary to popular belief, double-spaced copy is not always easier to read than single-spaced copy. Spacing should be dictated by the purpose and desired appearance of the report. However, single spaced paragraphs *must be* indented or separated with some blank space. A special desktop publishing advantage is the ability of the software to vary the line spacing–frequently called leading–versus leaving a single or double space.

Margins

Side, top and bottom margins should be one inch with the following exceptions. The first page of the body of the report should contain a top margin of approximately two inches. If the report is to be bound, additional room should be allowed for the binding.

Page Numbers

For ease of reading, the best location for page numbers is in the upper right corner. Page numbers can also be placed in the center of the page two lines below the last line. The first page is usually not numbered.

Listings/Enumerations

Many times a report is enhanced by the listing of points. If such a listing contains fairly short items, horizontal listing is appropriate. The following format applies for listing items horizontally: (a) use a colon before the list when it is preceded by a complete thought; (b) capitalize the first word of each item only when it is a proper noun, and (c) identify the listed items by enclosing either letters or numbers in parentheses.

Example 1–Modern

For longer listings, a listing or enumeration using a vertical format is more appropriate. The format is as follows:

Enumerations or listings use a bullet and are indented.

- Introduce a vertical listing with a complete thought.

- Double-space the first item, between items, and after the last item in the list.

- Indent the listed items five spaces from the left margin; and begin the second and succeeding lines of an item directly under the first word, not under the number.

Illustrations/Graphics

A picture is worth a thousand words! Therefore, illustrations and graphics make a report more complete and easier to read. They can be placed within the body of the report at the time they are mentioned or at the end of the report in an appendix. Illustrations and graphics should be used to illustrate a point, offer additional information, or emphasize a point. They should not be used simply for the sake of having something visual.

Quotations

Management reports rarely contain direct quotes. However, if a short quotation is desired, it is enclosed in quotation marks within the paragraph and referenced. The procedure for longer quotations is to indent about five spaces on both the left and the right sides.

References

Resources used in developing the report should be recognized in a bibliography. Specific quotes or paraphrases can be recognized by using either footnotes or endnotes. Endnotes appear at the end of the chapter, section, or report; footnotes appear at the bottom of the page. Because of the ease for both the reader and the writer, endnotes are frequently more popular in management reports. Endnotes are shown at the point of reference in the body, as follows: (Pearce, 1986). The complete reference appears in the bibliography.

Writing Style Elements

The normal rules of grammar, punctuation, and capitalization learned throughout the school years apply to all reports. In addition to the writing fundamentals, writing style is also important. Developing a clear and precise writing style that incorporates both personality and a professional attitude makes reading easier for your audience and more interesting! A concise book providing many rules (tried and proven) and principles of writing is *The Elements of Style* (Strunk and White, 1979).

Example 1–Modern

Person

Normally reports are written in third person in order to avoid the constant use of I, you, and we. If special emphasis is needed, usage of first or second person may be considered.

Parallel Construction

Related ideas should be stated in consistent or parallel form. This rule applies whether in an outline, in a series, in comparisons, in prepositional phrases, or with correlative expressions.

Subject/Verb Agreement

The subject and the verb of the sentence must agree with each other in number. For example, if a singular subject is used, a singular verb must be used.

Tense

Present tense should be used when an action is currently taking place; past tense is used to indicate previous action; and future tense indicates an action that will take place in the future. The appropriate tense should be chosen and used consistently throughout the report.

Expletives

Expletives do not contribute to meaning; they only fill space. Examples include these phrases: there are, this is, it is, and there are. Expletives are not grammatically incorrect, but the writer should be more specific in reports. The use of expletives tends to make the writing less clear and require a second reading.

Conclusion

Reports are a vital part of the business world. They can consume a great deal of time; but with application of the proper techniques, this time can be reduced and the quality of the reports improved. Productivity will increase for both the writer and reader if the developmental procedures, the format guidelines, and writing style elements of *The Five-Minute Report* are used.

Example 1–Modern

A bibliography page follows
the body. Note the hanging
indented format used.

Bibliography

Graves, Pat. R., and Murry, Jack E. "Enhancing Communication with Effective Page Design and Typography," *Instructional Strategies: An Applied Research Series*. Southwest Missouri State University, Springfield, Missouri: Delta Pi Epsilon, National Honorary Professional Graduate Society in Business Business 6:3, Summer, 1990.

Himstreet, William C., Wayne Murlin Baty, and Carol M. Lehman. *Business Communications: Principles and Methods (*10th ed.). Belmont, California: Wadsworth Publishing Company, 1993

Lundgren, Carol A. "Chapter 8. Building Communication Skills with Technologies," *Facilitating Communication for Business*, *NBEA Yearbook* No. 26. Reston, Virginia: National Business Education Association, 1988, pp. 72.

Mehren, Elizabeth. "Computers Redefining Publishing," *Los Angeles Times*, (January 3, 1994), E6.

Pauley, Steven E., and Daniel G. Riordan. *Technical Report Writing Today*. 4th ed. Boston: Houghton Mifflin Company, 1987.

Pearce, C. Glenn. "Business Writing: Computer Instruction vs. Traditional Methods." *Business Education Forum* 40: 11-12, May 1986.

Strunk, William and E. B. White. *The Elements of Style*. New York: Macmillan Publishing Company, Inc., 1979.

Vik, Gretchen N., Wilkinson, Clyde W., and Wilkinson, Dorothy C. *Writing and Speaking in Business*. Boston: Irwin, 1990.

Example 2–Ultra-Modern

Note: The nine-page report is reduced to five pages. The main differences between this report and the **Example 1–Modern** are the boxed headings using reverse type, the two-column format, and the drop caps.

Example 3–Enhanced Modern

Note: This example is similar to **Example 2–Ultra-Modern** but it also incorporates the use of images to help the reader visualize the information in the report. Images can be photographs, clip art, drawings, charts or graphs, or quotations (called "pull quotes" and set aside from the copy with ruled lines).

Example 4–Traditional

Note: This example has the same content as the others. It utilizes headings and subheadings. However, the report could have been produced on a typewriter rather than a computer.

Outlining

Appendix C

How to Write Structurally Sound Text

by William H. Baker
Department of Management Communication
Brigham Young University
Provo, Utah

Before you write a document, you should create an outline to guide your writing. The text in Appendix C explains how to prepare an outline and how to evaluate the outline to be sure it is complete and structurally sound.

Prepare an Outline

Write the Title

The first step in creating an outline is to write the title, which defines the subject matter of the document. The title must accurately describe what the text is all about. For the planning phase, use a *functional* title rather than a creative, attention-getting title. For example, use *Why XYZ Corporation Should Build a New Shipping Facility in Atlanta*, rather than *Atlanta: City of Growth*. A functional title is helpful in reminding you of the document's objective.

Determine the Categories

The material you write in your text should be divided into relatively small pieces for easier reading. Therefore, you need to determine the *categories* into which the text can later be *classified*. For example, a written proposal to change the location where employees of a company may park their cars might include categories like (a) Current Policy, (b) Proposed Policy, (c) Advantages of the Proposed Policy, and (d) Implementation Procedures. The names of these categories can be used later as headings (i.e., titles) of the various parts of the report.

Depending on the length of the text you are planning to write, the main categories could be subdivided into even smaller subcategories. Longer documents need more categories, such as Introduction, Analysis, and Conclusion; while a shorter document might have six main categories with one or more levels of subcategories under each of the six main categories.

For example, an outline for a document describing 500 major tourist sites in the Western United States would be somewhat overwhelming if the sites were simply listed from 1 to 500. An improvement would be to group the sites by state (Arizona, California, Oregon, etc.). Further within each state the sites could be grouped according to type (Historic Buildings, Parks, Resorts, etc.). The resulting outline would thus have three levels of categories under the title, as follows:

Title: The 500 Most Popular Tourist Sites in the
Western United States
Level 1 Categories: Arizona, California, Nevada, etc.
Level 2 Categories: Historic Buildings, National
Parks, Resorts, etc.
Level 3 Categories: Names of the specific
tourist sites

Thus, Zion Canyon would be a subcategory of National Parks, which would be a subcategory of Utah, which would be a subcategory of the title (The 500 Most Popular Tourist Sites in the Western United States). Even within the Zion Canyon category, you could have additional subdivisions, such as Accommodations, Map, Fees, Weather, etc.

Organize the Categories

Hierarchy. Different levels of categories must be organized into a hierarchy, with the title being at the top of the hierarchy. In the hierarchy, the various levels of categories and subcategories should be indented and identified according to the following pattern:

Title
   I.   First first-level category
       A.   First second-level subcategory
          1.   First third-level subcategory
             a.   First fourth-level subcategory
               (1) First fifth-level subcategory

(a) First sixth-level subcategory
(b) Second sixth-level subcategory
(2) Second fifth-level subcategory
b. Second fourth-level subcategory
2. Second third-level subcategory
B. Second second-level subcategory
II. Second first-level category

Using this approach, an outline with two levels (I, II, etc., and A, B, etc.) may appear as follows:

Title: Results of Management Audit of Administrative
Services Division
I. Introduction
II. Information Services
A. Computer Systems
B. Records Management
III. Human Resources Department
A. Employment
B. Benefits
C. Training and Development
IV. Accounting
V. Accounts Payable
VI. Accounts Receivable
VII. Marketing
A. Advertising
B. Sales
VIII. Conclusions and Recommendations

Sequence. In addition to the hierarchical organization, each module must be sequenced appropriately. Categories can be considered as one of two types: *nouns* (person, place, thing, or idea) or *verbs* (actions or events). Noun categories tell about something at a specific point in time; they include such descriptions as who, what, why, and where. Verb categories describe something that moves or changes over a period of time; they involve time-sequence information, such as when each of several events occurred or how to perform the steps in a procedure.

Noun categories are sequenced according to *quantity* (e.g., more before less), *quality* (e.g., better before worse), *space* (e.g., high before low), *alphabet* (e.g., A before B), or some other comparative or otherwise logical measure. *Verb* categories are usually arranged chronologically according to *order of occurrence:* sooner before later (e.g., procedure 1 before procedure 2, cause before effect, stimulus before response, problem before solution, question before answer).

Noun Category example (sequenced from highest to lowest quality):

> *Comparison* of the Top Three Job Finalists
> - Chris Gudeman
> - Pat Robinson
> - Kim Martin

Verb Category example (sequenced according to the order in which the steps must be performed):

> How to Perform the Inventory Tagging Process
> - Receive purchase notification
> - Assign inventory ID number
> - Create ID tag
> - Place ID tag on inventory item

Evaluate the Outline

After the outline is completed, evaluate it to make sure it is structurally sound. To perform the evaluation, use a procedure known as STEP (Structured-Text Evaluation Procedure). STEP consists of evaluating each *module*, or group of categories, starting at the first-level categories and then progressing module by module to the most detailed level of the hierarchy. (A module is one group of parallel categories, such as I, II, III or A, B, C, D. Each occurrence of a I, A, 1, a, (1), or (a) in an outline signifies the first item in a module.)

Using STEP, you conduct five tests on each module as follows:

1. *Inclusion* (or presence) test: Given the title or heading of a module, are all appropriate items included? If not, restrict the scope of the title or heading to fit the items that are present, or add the missing items. Make sure that every module contains at least two items (e.g., A *and* B or 1 *and* 2).

2. *Exclusion* (or absence) test: Given the title or heading of a module, are all inappropriate items excluded? If not, delete the inappropriate items, or expand the title or heading to fit all the items in the module.

3. *Hierarchy* (or horizontal) test: Are the items in the module hierarchically parallel? If not, shift the problem items to the appropriate level (e.g., from the A, B, C level to the 1, 2, 3 level), and make other adjustments necessary to ensure hierarchical parallelism. In most cases there is no specific right or wrong hierarchy, because most subject matter can be organized in a variety of ways. The writer must decide which organization seems most logical in each circumstance.

4. *Sequence* (or vertical) test: Are the items in the appropriate sequence? Determine whether the module is of the noun or verb type, and then decide which sequence seems to be most appropriate for each module. Be sure to make this determination from the standpoint of helping the reader.

5. *Language* (or wording) test: Are the items in the module grammatically parallel? If not, change the wording to achieve parallelism. (This test is important only if the items are used as headings or subheadings in the final text. If they are not, skip this test.)

These tests can be easily remembered by thinking of the words *presence, absence, horizontal, vertical,* and *wording.*

The following example shows how the STEP tests are performed on the first module (first-level categories) of the *Results of Management Audit of Administrative Services Division* outline.

STEP Test 1 (Inclusion Test):

Results of Management Audit of Administrative Services Division
- I.   Introduction
- II.   Information Services
- III. Human Resources Department
- IV.   Accounting
- V.   Accounts Payable
- VI.   Accounts Receivable
- VII. Marketing
- VIII. Conclusions and Recommendations

Are all units in the Administrative Services Division present? No, the Purchasing Department, a small department with no subunits within it, is missing and needs to be included.

STEP Test 2 (Exclusion Test):

Results of Management Audit of Administrative Services Division
- I.   Introduction
- II.   Information Services
- III. Human Resources Department
- IV.   Accounting
- V.   Accounts Payable
- VI.   Accounts Receivable
- VII. Marketing
- VIII. Purchasing
- IX.   Conclusions and Recommendations

Are all units in the Administrative Services Division present? Yes, Marketing is not part of the Administrative Services Division and should be excluded.

STEP Test 3 (Hierarchy Test):

Results of Management Audit of Administrative Services Division

I.	Introduction
II.	Information Services
III.	Human Resources Department
IV.	Accounting
V.	Accounts Payable
VI.	Accounts Receivable
VII.	Purchasing
VIII.	Conclusions and Recommendations

Are all the items in the module hierarchically parallel (on the right level)? No, Accounts Payable and Accounts Receivable are divisions of Accounting. Therefore, they should be shifted to the second level as subdivisions A and B under Accounting and be tested as a separate module.

STEP Test 4 (Sequence Test):

Results of Management Audit of Administrative Services Division

I.	Introduction
II.	Information Services
III.	Human Resources Department
IV.	Accounting
	A. Accounts Payable
	B. Accounts Receivable
V.	Purchasing
VI.	Conclusions and Recommendations

Are all the items in the most appropriate sequence? This module is a *noun*-type module; therefore, it will not be arranged in a time sequence. Items I and VI are arranged in the order in which we want the reader to encounter them in the report. Items II–V could be arranged by order of size (e.g., largest to smallest) or by order of management problems identified in the audit (e.g., most to least). However, an alphabetic arrangement seems to be more appropriate.

STEP Test 5 (Language Test):

Results of Management Audit of Administrative Services Division
    I.   Introduction
    II.   Accounting
          A. Accounts Payable
          B. Accounts Receivable
    III.   Human Resources Department
    IV.   Information Services
    V.   Purchasing
    VI.   Conclusions and Recommendations

Are all the items parallel in language? No, items II, III, IV, and V are departments, but only item III includes the word *Department*. Therefore, *Department* should be added to items II, IV, and V.

The Revised Outline

With all the necessary changes made, module *I-VI* now passes all five tests:

Results of Management Audit of Administrative Services Division
    I.   Introduction
    II.   Accounting Department
          A. Accounts Payable
          B. Accounts Receivable
    III.   Human Resources Department
          A. Employment
          B. Benefits
          C. Training and Development
    IV.   Information Services Department
          A. Computer Systems
          B. Records Management
    V.   Purchasing Department
    VI.   Conclusions and Recommendations

After the tests are completed on the first module, they are repeated on all remaining modules. For this example, you would next complete the STEP tests on the three remaining modules in the following order: (a) II, A-B; (b) III, A-C; and (c) IV, A-B. (Note: This structure might change during the evaluation process, resulting in either more or fewer modules to be tested.)

If there were additional levels of submodules, they would be identified and tested in the same manner. For example, if Employment had two subdivisions, it would be identified as module III, A, 1-2 and would be tested after module III, A-C.

Figure 1 illustrates the STEP Report Form used to record the test results of each module. This form is particularly useful when you evaluate the structure of another person's writing. Usually, the other person will give you just the text without a Table of Contents or outline. When this occurs, briefly scan the text (headings, topic sentences, etc.) and create an outline as you go. Then complete the STEP tests on all the modules in the outline you have created; record your evaluations on the STEP Report Form; and give appropriate feedback to the writer.

Conclusion

The STEP procedure is a comprehensive, yet relatively simple, writing tool. The five STEP tests encompass every type of change you can make in an outline: (1) addition, (2) deletion, (3) horizontal movement, (4) vertical movement, and (5) change of wording. Tests 1 and 2 help ensure that the proper *content* is included in each module; tests 3 and 4 make sure the items are properly *placed* (horizontally and vertically), and test 5 guarantees proper *language* parallelism.

Four important benefits come from faithfully using the STEP tests. First, the tests help ensure the structural soundness of text. Second, they also help produce clearer thinking. These tests methodically challenge your thought processes, helping assure that no content or organizational considerations are overlooked. Third, the STEP process helps you compose text more efficiently–writing becomes a straight-forward process of expanding the outline, rather than a perplexing process of not knowing what to write next. Fourth, your text will be easier to read and understand. And that is something readers greatly appreciate.

STEP Report Form

Title: Results of Management Audit
              of Administrative Services Division

Author: John Doe

Module: <u>Title, I-VIII</u>
1. Presence   Add *Purchasing.*
2. Absence   Eliminate *Marketing.*
3. Hierarchy   Put *Accounts Payable* and *Accounts Receivable*
                       as subdivisions of *Accounting.*
4. Sequence   Arrange in alphabetical order.
5. Language   Add the word *Department* to items II, IV, and
                       V.

Module: <u>II, A-B</u>
1. Presence   Add *Payroll* and *Budget.*
2. Absence   ok
3. Hierarchy   ok
4. Sequence   Arrange in alphabetical order.
5. Language   ok

Module: <u>III, A-C</u>
1. Presence   ok
2. Absence   ok
3. Hierarchy   ok
4. Sequence   Arrange in alphabetical order.
5. Language   ok

Module: <u>IV, A-B</u>
1. Presence   Add *Reproduction Services.*
2. Absence   ok
3. Hierarchy   ok
4. Sequence   ok
5. Language   ok

Figure 1. The STEP Report Form, showing changes previously made in the first module and changes that should be made in the other three modules.

The Final Outline

STEP Report Form

Title: Results of Management Audit
          of Administrative Services Division

Author: John Doe

I.   Introduction

II. Accounting Department
     A. Accounts Payable
     B. Accounts Receivable
     C. Budget
     D. Payroll

III. Human Resources Department
     A. Benefits
     B. Employment
     C. Training and Development

IV. Information Services Department
     A. Computer Systems
     B. Records Management
     C. Reproduction Services

V.   Purchasing Department

VI. Conclusions and Recommendations

Index